O9-ABH-802

Twayne's United States Authors Series

Sylvia E. Bowman, *Editor*

INDIANA UNIVERSITY

Marianne Moore

MARIANNE MOORE

by

BERNARD F. ENGEL

The poetry of Marianne Moore is almost unique in our times for its willingness to assert principles of ethics. Though bad poets have been all too willing to rush in with easy answers to difficult questions, most of our good poets have felt the times to be too out-of-joint for statements of ethics. Miss Moore is a first-rate poet who believes that certain values persist regardless of the times; she has with scrupulous care found, investigated, and presented in brilliantly witty poetry instances of the courage, naturalness, and spontaneity she values. In so doing she has complied with the credo of Walt Whitman and T. S. Eliot that the true poet, though he must write poems rather than versified sermons, will ultimately be a critic of ethics.

This first full-length book on Miss Moore and her poetry traces her development from the early assertions of the values of courageous individualism as exemplified in animals and objects. It finds that she moved to declarations of a need for man to recognize "as ifs" in existence, and to the decision that one should armor himself not merely for protection from the world but also for usefulness within it. It shows that in her latest period she has come to assert a unity of spirit and appearance, to hope for a vision, and to meditate on a need for redemption and resurrection. Thus in her early work the hero is the aloof, isolated individual who survives the shock waves the world hurls against him; in her latest poems the hero is the unaccommodating but blessed man, pacific yet passionate, who achieves a salvation enabling him to create art.

Professor Engel begins with an example of Miss Moore's procedures, briefly sets forth the facts of her biography—including an account of an interview in her Brooklyn apartment—and then gives a poem-by-poem elucidation of her development as an esthetician of ethics. The book therefore is not only the first full-length study of one of the major poets of our time; it is also a handbook and guide to individual poems.

MARIANNE MOORE

by **BERNARD F. ENGEL**

Michigan State University

CARNEGIE LIBRARY
LIVINGSTONE COLLEGE
SALISBURY. N. C. 28144

Twayne Publishers, Inc.   ::   New York

Copyright © 1964 by Twayne Publishers, Inc.

All Rights Reserved

Library of Congress Catalog Card Number: 63-20613

MANUFACTURED IN THE UNITED STATES OF AMERICA BY
UNITED PRINTING SERVICES, INC.
NEW HAVEN, CONN.

811.52
En 57

10-8-69 -Direct-14/50

To Adele
WIFE AND PARTNER

4·76 00

Preface

MOST OF US in the twentieth century give obeisance to one version or another of Archibald MacLeish's famous dictum that a poem must not mean but be. The best known comment upon Marianne Moore's work, T. S. Eliot's introduction to her *Selected Poems,* remarks that it would be hard to say what is the subject matter of her poem "The Jerboa." And Miss Moore herself has at times spoken as though she too believes in what some idealize as a pure poetry, one removed from and beyond mundane concern with subject and statement. MacLeish, Eliot, and Miss Moore are formidable authorities. But more than one critical precept has become critical cant. Perhaps over the past generation we have been suffering a hangover of Romanticism, a reaction against excessive claims of goody-goody gray Victorians that has caused us in public pronouncements to admire a "pure" art that few poets actually write.

Miss Moore's poetry certainly *means,* and not only in senses that would suit the authors of *Theory of Literature.* She herself admits concern with statement, as when in "Idiosyncrasy and Technique" she confesses that the genesis of the poem "Blessed Is the Man" was a desire to correct scoffers. She even, in the Foreword to *A Marianne Moore Reader,* admits that the term moralist is appropriate for her. In the 1960's it should no longer be necessary to be coy about the plain fact that in her poetry she is indeed an examiner and affirmer of values. The last-ditch defender of the "pure" could argue that statement of ethics is only a device for obtaining rhetorical coherence, what the composition handbooks call a "central point." But this too would be coy. Her poems typically not only assert in a fairly direct manner an opinion on ethics; they usually also are suffused throughout with attitudes of approval or distaste reinforcing that point.

Her values are in themselves conventional. They emphasize independence, courage, fortitude, and endurance, suggesting a belief that this world offers a hard and sparse existence.

She told the editors of *Twentieth Century Authors* that she honors the family, unselfishness, and "freedom for all races and persons." Her responses to a *Partisan Review* symposium on religion show that she is Emersonian enough to insist that preservation of the individual is primary, that self-discipline therefore is the fundamental necessity from which any social discipline must arise. Her belief is persistent enough for her to maintain that science and religion are compatible, that "diligence"—human reason—is not capable of solving all mystery. Especially in her later work she is sometimes specifically Christian, expressing a yearning for a resurrection and viewing sacrifice as a means to redemption.

She is occasionally a moralist in quite direct ways. Thus in her essay "If I Were Sixteen Today" she writes in favor of such virtues as promptness and chastity, as well as of the silence that, she says, can "make possible promptings from on high." And William Carlos Williams, writing to Robert Lowell in 1951 of troubles with women editors and readers, complained that Miss Moore took him severely to task because Book four of his long poem *Paterson* deals with a Lesbian. None of this is esoteric. Miss Moore's virtues as a poet lie not in novelty or rebellion but in ability to "make it new," to give a poetic realization that restores life to values often served more by lip than by mind and energy.

For these reasons I have not hesitated to trace the plot or line of argument in a poem, to give what is sometimes a paraphrase, and to remark upon a poem's statement. I hereby swear what should be an unnecessary oath: I do not believe that paraphrase and commentary exhaust the possibilities of a poem.

Miss Moore had the advice of Ezra Pound that the order of presentation in a book of poems is important; and she had the aid of T. S. Eliot in establishing the order in *Selected Poems*. Because of these counselors' authority and because it seems most convenient for the reader, I have considered her poems in the order in which they appear in her several books. Intending to produce a companion to her poems, not a substitute for them, I have deliberately kept quotation short.

Acknowledgments

Miss Moore has been a warmly courteous hostess to me and also has given sprightly, generous, and prompt answers to my letters. But she has not seen the manuscript of this book, and is not responsible for either its statements of fact or its opinions.

I wish to thank her for granting permission to quote from her published works. I also want to thank Michigan State University for all-university research grants that covered some expenses of preparing the manuscript. Portions of Chapter I are revised from an essay I read at the 1962 meeting of the Language and Literature section, Michigan Academy of Sciences, Arts, and Letters; the essay was printed in Volume XLVIII of the Academy's *Papers*. Janet M. Agnew, head librarian of Bryn Mawr College, furnished copies of Miss Moore's poetry in student publications.

Contents

Chronology

1887   Born November 15 in Kirkwood, near St. Louis, Missouri.

1894   After death of grandfather, mother moves family to Carlisle, Pennsylvania.

1896-   Educated at Carlisle's Metzger schools.
1905

1905-   Student at Bryn Mawr College, Bryn Mawr, Pennsylva-
1909   nia; B.A., 1909. First published poetry appears in Bryn Mawr's *Tipyn O' Bob* and *The Lantern*.

1910   Student at Carlisle Commercial College.

1911   Visits Europe.

1911-   Teacher of commercial subjects at United States Indian
1915   School, Carlisle.

1915   First professional publication, "To the Soul of Progress," in *The Egoist* (London); five poems in *Poetry*. Begins to win reputation as one of "new" poets.

1916   With her mother, moves to Chatham, New Jersey, to keep house for her brother John, assigned there as Presbyterian minister.

1918   Her brother John joining the navy for World War I service as chaplain, Miss Moore and her mother move to Manhattan apartment where they live for eleven years. In next year or two, employed as secretary in a girls' school and as a private tutor.

1920   First of her group to appear in *The Dial*, confirming recognition of her as a major innovator.

1921-   Employed as assistant in New York Public Library.
1925

1921   *Poems*, published by The Egoist Press, London.

1922   Harriet Monroe symposium, in *Poetry*, on Miss Moore's work indicates her prominence.

1923   "Marriage" published separately.

1924 *Observations.*

1925 Receives Dial Award for 1924; five consecutive issues of *The Dial* laud her work, and she becomes acting editor beginning with the July issue. For next four years she is active with the magazine and publishes no verse of her own.

1926 Appointed editor of *The Dial,* beginning with July issue.

1929 Publication of *The Dial* ends with July issue; Miss Moore leaves Manhattan for the Brooklyn apartment that is still her home. Begins career as free-lance poet, book reviewer, writer of occasional articles.

1932 Helen Haire Levinson Prize signifies her return to prominence as active poet.

1935 *Selected Poems;* Ernest Hartsock Memorial Prize.

1936 *The Pangolin and Other Verse.*

1940 Shelley Memorial Award.

1941 *What Are Years.*

1944 *Nevertheless.* Contemporary Poetry's Patrons' Prize; Harriet Monroe Poetry Award.

1945 Guggenheim Fellowship in creative writing. Translator, with Elizabeth Mayer, of Adalbert Stifter's *Rock Crystal, A Christmas Tale.*

1946 Joint grant of $1,000 from American Academy of Arts and Letters and National Institute of Arts and Letters. Begins translation of La Fontaine's *Fables.*

1947 Elected to National Institute of Arts and Letters.

1949 "A Face" published separately. First of many honorary degrees, a Litt.D. from Wilson College.

1950 Honorary degrees from Mount Holyoke College and from Smith College.

1951 *Collected Poems;* honorary degree from University of Rochester.

1952 *Annus mirabilis:* National Book Award for poetry, Pulitzer Prize for poetry, and Bollingen Prize. Honorary degree from Dickinson College, Youth Oscar Award from Brooklyn's Youth United for a Better Tomorrow.

1953 Gold Medal for Poetry, National Institute of Arts and Letters; honorary degree, Long Island University; visiting lecturer, Bryn Mawr; M. Carey Thomas Award.

1954 *The Fables of La Fontaine; Gedichte* (bilingual edition of poems, published in Germany).

1955 *Predilections* (selected essays); *Selected Fables;* honorary degree from Douglass College of Rutgers University.

1956 *Like a Bulwark.*

1958 Honorary degree from Pratt Institute.

1959 *O to Be a Dragon.*

1961 *A Marianne Moore Reader.*

1962 *The Absentee.*

1963 *Puss in Boots, The Sleeping Beauty,* and *Cinderella*

CHAPTER 1

Poet and Person

F ASCINATION WITH PARADOX is the most immediately
striking aspect of the verse of Marianne Moore. Her famous
counsel in "Poetry" that poets should present "imaginary gardens
with real toads in them," should be "literalists of the imagination,"
bewilders the undergraduate as it bemuses the critic. This
interest in the seemingly contradictory is often witty and, at
times, playful (the garden is populated not with humming-
birds and butterflies but with "real toads"). But it is also
profound. Paradox is of the essence of her work because she
wishes to advocate a set of values; yet as an artist and as a
person she adheres to principles that enjoin caution in assertion.

The values she would advocate are those of what she terms
morality, a morality that, she told a *Partisan Review* symposium,[1]
is "self-demonstrating." They are those values that inspire decency
as a member of a community and—more emphasized—those
that she believes lead to honor as an individual. They include
courage, independence, responsibility, genuineness, and a certain
ardor in the conduct of one's life. Presentation of this ethics
is built into her work. Her subject matter is whatever is experienced, whether through the senses or by the imagination. Since
she does not believe experience to be ethically neutral, her presentation would be less than complete if it omitted meditation
upon values.

I *The Alone Distinction of Merit: Objectivism*

If Miss Moore were living in the confident eighteenth century,
the age of the reasonable abstraction, she might argue her
values directly. But Miss Moore works in a tradition that
respects inductive methods. This is the tradition of, for example,
William Blake, who wrote that "To Generalize is to be an Idiot.
To Particularize is the Alone Distinction of Merit," and that

"Without Minute Neatness of Execution The Sublime cannot Exist!" Belief that the artist can cause transmutation of accumulated particulars into a sublimity that is more than the sum of its parts is a romantic faith linking Blake to Ezra Pound, to William Carlos Williams, and of course to Marianne Moore.

Miss Moore's preaching therefore has been restrained. She has sought to illustrate and prove her convictions by careful selection of exact details to realize the particularities of an object. This she believes will make her presentation convincing to the reader who, it is assumed, will obstinately refuse to believe what our era calls a "mere" abstraction. In its focus upon the object her method is associated with principles of the Objectivism sponsored by Louis Zukofsky in the 1920's. Zukofsky rejected the term "movement" for his activities, and these were so short-lived and, indeed, so informal that such a term for them would be grandiose. Though his Objectivism was scarcely a new principle, it is worth recalling because it aroused theoretical consideration of practices employed by Wallace Stevens as well as by Miss Moore. Zukofsky's own not always coherent remarks in *An "Objectivists" Anthology* (1932) defined the "objective" as that which is aimed at, and Objective poetry thus as that which is "objectively perfect, inextricably the direction of historical and contemporary particulars"; he recommended Miss Moore's poem "An Egyptian Pulled-glass Bottle in the Shape of a Fish" and her early book *Observations* as examples.

Other commentators have more usually meant by Objectivism a focus on a concrete object—on what Stevens and Williams hail as "the thing itself." Ideas supposedly have no existence independent from the circumstances in which they are found and which, so the belief is, have given rise to them. The poet therefore should set down in rigorous precision a selection of observed details of the "thing," the object or objects that he believes to be inextricably associated with whatever idea he may be working to present. Such a technique would seem to limit severely the poet's ability to comment upon ideas larger than the minutiae of immediate perception; in fact, however, neither Stevens nor Williams limited his work in line with the slogans of Objectivism. Even Williams' famous Objectivist poem "The Red Wheel-barrow" suggests significances in its remark that "so much depends/upon" the object.

Though Miss Moore uses the rigorously perceived detail, she is even less limited than Williams and Stevens to the "thing"—to the data accessible to the senses. It is true that when writing of an apple, for example, she will try to give, as Williams put it admiringly in a *Dial* review, "the hard and unaffected concept of the apple itself as an idea, then its edge to edge contact with the things which surround it." What surrounds it, however, is not only a world of orchards, but one of brilliantly imagined connections and connotations, a world where apple trees mingle with caterpillars and pangolins and glaciers, with courages and voracities and ironies.

Her grounds for faith in Objectivism, of course, are not those of Williams. His belief may be described as scientific, a faith that values are inherent in objects because all are parts of the phenomenal world in which both reason and imagination begin. But Miss Moore believes in the existence of a spiritual world. To her, objects are important because they are or contain something more than the qualities of mere phenomena. To see the thing itself is to Williams a process of reduction, of stripping away to an essence believed to provide a base on which man may build an ethic more valid than the outworn, fraudulent systems of the twentieth century. But to Miss Moore it is a process of expansion, a discarding of mundanities to release a spiritual self. Belief in the existence of a spiritual understructure to the world of appearances gives her confidence in the rightness of her devotion to presentation of the object. As she says in "He 'Digesteth Harde Yron,'" the power of the visible is "the invisible"; by specifying exact details the poet can "dramatize a/meaning always missed/by the externalist." The object, the freshly perceived "thing," has power to suggest or convey meaning by being its exact self because its selfhood—when seen clearly—is not narrowed from but is expanded beyond its physical outlines. To find the self is not to discover an irreducible stone of true being hidden inside a mass of the irrelevant and false. It is rather to throw a stone into a pool: it is to note the rings of meaning which widen around and beyond the self when it is set in motion.

Concern with both ethics and "things" has made Miss Moore frequently a poet of the analogy: she presents the "thing" in order to suggest or assert a point of ethics. And even though meanings arise from the object, she is not averse to tucking a "moral" into a poem to make sure that her point will be plain. Sometimes, both in such relatively early work as "The Jerboa" and "The Plumet Basilisk" and in such later pieces as "The Arctic Ox," she is so charmed by the creature she is presenting that the delight she communicates is in itself the chief conveyer of meaning. Even in these poems, however, there are bits of overt statement, significant juxtapositions, and other signposts for the reader.

But a poet so earnest in advocacy of values may also be expected to break into direct commentary, and this Miss Moore has sometimes done. To the critic who values metaphor in one form or another as the very essence of poetry, her practice seems at times too editorial. Roy Harvey Pearce, for example, in *The Continuity of American Poetry* doubts that such of her work as "What Are Years?" is poetry at all. Miss Moore's admirers obviously believe that she has succeeded in making commentary function as presentation, that she knows just how much delineation of the "thing" is needed to honey the lip of the cup.

She is, then, a poet to whom imagination is fundamental. Such a poet is frequently egocentric: we hear always of the emotions Shelley, Keats, and Wordsworth had when confronted with a skylark, urn, or daffodil. Objectivism is one strategy enabling Miss Moore to keep her eye on the object. Another tactic for adherence to the thing itself is restraint, what critics call her "armoring." She must guard against intrusions of conventional feeling: hence, for example, her frequent selection of exotic animals and other "things" that her reader is not likely to have preconceptions about. She wants to avoid reference to her private life and, usually, to her own political and social opinions. Desire for such restraint demands of her the self-sufficiency to explore fresh subject matter, and it reinforces her insistence on the self-discipline that will enable her to adhere to her subject.

She has often commented, in both prose and verse, upon the difficulties of her mode. One of her early poetic considerations of paradox, ethics, and problems of communication is in the poem "Melanchthon" (originally "Black Earth"), which is neither so compact nor so precise as the best of her work. But it is a good example of her effort to use analogy without being dominated by it, and it also gives strong, overt statement of faith in the existence of a power underlying and superior to the appearances of life in this world.

The poem is presented as a first-person meditation on the failure of its speaker to achieve reforms, a failure seen as owing to inability to communicate her ideas. Its use of feminine pronouns to refer to this speaker is proper, for in the context of her work the poem's style, temperament, and concerns are such that it would be unnecessarily coy to assume that the speaker is anyone other than Miss Moore herself. The later title "Melanchthon" is Greek for "black earth," and may refer to dark spirits of the underworld. "Melanchthon" also translates the last name of Philipp Schwarzert and is commonly applied to him. He was a German Reformation leader who wished to reconcile differences between Catholics and Protestants. Perhaps Miss Moore, in indirectly using his name, is indicating desire to reform without being divisive. Certainly there is some allusion to the idea of beauty under darkness mentioned in the Song of Solomon (where, in the King James translation, the speaker refers to herself as "black, but comely"), an idea sometimes taken to be a metaphor descriptive of the human body in its role as container of the soul.[2]

Failure to communicate is not owing to secretiveness. Indeed, so the poem's first stanzas tell us, natural openness is one of the speaker's primary characteristics. The hippopotamus and the alligator who alternately bathe and sun themselves along the jungle stream represent the independent-minded, tough-skinned beings Miss Moore favors. Like these creatures, the speaker wants to experience phenomena, not to examine or to be intellectual about them. And like them, she does what she does to please herself; she acts without subterfuge.

Living in open naturalness the speaker can say that, like the aquatic creature whose guise she temporarily assumes, "now I breathe and now I am submerged." Such an animal is sometimes knobbed and horned; as on his hide, so in her work the "blemishes" stand out and she, being honest, will not "say the contrary." She has failed to achieve the "renaissance" she worked for. This failure arises, paradoxically, from her very naturalness; for submergence, even that in poetry and values, of course conceals. But concealment, the failure to communicate success-fully, is not only a result of particular activities. It is the inevit-able lot of the human, cloaked as she necessarily is in a material body. Part of this physical superstructure is a product of the times; but if this "sediment" which encrusts her were to be done away with, she says, some part of her would be gone. We may note that the deposit is not filth or slime but a "patina," for it enriches what was "there to begin with." There is, then, at the core of the individual an "I," a self that is prior to all the layers of material structure in which during life in this world it is enwrapped. Yet this "I" is not entirely separate from its physical body; it is in part shaped by, is to some degree the product of, its experiences in this world.

The exterior of the "I" may also be represented as black glass, inscribed by the individual's experiences so that it has become a text from which the ignorant might learn something of the effects of encounters with "power." Real "power," however, does not lie in the experiences which have scarred the body. It is that influence, that strength represented by what here is termed the "soul." Throughout her existence, the speaker says, her comprehension of "life and death" has been limited to what her senses could tell her; yet she understands that there are "feats of strength" whose sources are not detectable by the senses. Though her soul will never be wounded by material weapons, she is "on . . . guard"; for she cannot know wholly what to expect from the realm not accessible to the senses. This stance of the "I," this guardedness, amounts to a "spiritual poise" whose exact source cannot be known. Yet the "I" can "see" and "hear" to depths the body cannot perceive. The body—here represented as being, like the elephant's trunk, "wandlike" and a "tree-trunk without roots"—is kept whole only by material forces and is in its opacity akin to the coral which misrepresents whatever "light" it may receive.

Through the first thirteen stanzas of "Melanchthon," then, we are told that the complete human being has both soul and body, that both are part of the self, but that the soul, the central "I," comes from and responds to sources deeper than those detectable by the body. This body, unavoidably an accompaniment of the life of the self in this world, consequently is limited in understanding; it conceals much of the true self, and its perceptions are exceedingly clumsy. The result is that the "I" of each one of us can communicate to the "I" of any other individual in only a "fretful," an imperfect, less than truly revelatory speech. Therefore, we may deduce, the failure of the artist to achieve more than a partial victory is inevitable.

Yet we are not to be contemptuous of this "elephant," this clumsy body which conceals as much as it reveals. Though somewhat gross, it is not merely "black earth"; and though it is susceptible to the spears of harsh experience, it can hold off at least some of the darts of adversity. It demonstrates, the speaker says somewhat playfully, just how "indestructible" matter is. And, she says more seriously, it endures shocks and upheavals which would put an end to lesser phenomena. It has, after all, a depth to it, the depth given it by the soul it harbors. In phrasing her ending assertion as a question, Miss Moore shows her confidence that she has guided her reader to an understanding of the nature and relationship of body and soul. Would the "depth," the significance of an individual be visible to one who did not recognize the "beautiful element of unreason" in him? The question is of course an affirmation, for by suggesting the blindness of him who refuses to see the soul Miss Moore asserts her belief in the existence of such a spiritual core to the self.

The problem of communication and expression thus arises from the nature of the human being. Encased in a serviceable but less than perfect body, the central "I" of the individual can never make known more than a limited portion of itself to the "I" of another individual. It is hardly to be expected that reform in ethics, in value systems, can be wholly achieved when one recognizes the difficulty of communicating his perceptions. The "black earth" we all bear is in this life a necessary armor; yet, in blocking the shafts that would wound, it also bars the light that would save.

Since Miss Moore frequently recommends that the individual maintain a certain distance from his fellows, a poised and dignified independence, we may assume that she thinks the price not too heavy. When shut off to some degree from others, we cannot fully comprehend nor be comprehended by them; yet only such separateness can enable us to adopt that cliff-like stance of independence she advises. We may deduce that the dichotomy of soul and body, of spiritual and material, gives rise to those paradoxes which Miss Moore sees neither as quaint or clever absurdities, nor as tragic flaws, but as inevitabilities of human experience. Miss Moore herself chooses to view a paradox not as a problem to be solved but as a situation to be explored for significances. In this exploration arises her poem, whether as a record of discovery or as a report of a search in progress.

II *Achievement of Distinction: Tactics of Style*

The most obvious characteristic of Miss Moore's style is discipline. In "Melanchthon," for example, the argument, the intended statement, directs the movement throughout. Yet the verse is never allowed to soar far from reference to a concrete object, whether animal, glass, or coral; no system of analogy, no over-all metaphor, is permitted to assume governance, to lure the poem away from its particulars. The rhetorical form is that of a series of questions, but by inversion and by careful placement these are subdued to avoid prose-like obviousness. The poem's deliberate, declarative tone is further guarded by the use of seemingly subordinate *which*-clauses to advance assertions and by the linking of series of statements with semicolons instead of with conjunctions to give an effect of factual assertion. Rhyme is present in the first two lines of each stanza, but is de-emphasized so as to avoid musicality; the meter, based on careful counting of syllables, also is intended to support the guise of reasoned statement.

The poem admits neither ungrounded interpretations of the esthetic data nor obvious ornament. The desired effect is that of careful deliberation, serious but not grim, and conversational rather than flatly argumentative. The style, that is, exemplifies the restraint that Miss Moore values.

The rhetoric and style of "Melanchthon" are representative, but are by no means the only tactics Miss Moore employs. She can vary from the directly editorial ("Marriage") to the celebratory ("The Jerboa," "The Plumet Basilisk") and the deliberately ponderous ("To a Steamroller"). She is nearly always witty, and sometimes exploits devices of wit to develop an entire poem; examples are "For February 14th," depending on reversal of expectations, and "Carnegie Hall: Rescued," setting up a proposition in order to demolish it. In her meditative, exploratory mood, she may, as in "Armour's Undermining Modesty," begin with seeming casualness and move by apparently whimsical juxtapositions to investigate calmly now one, now another aspect of her topic until she arrives at a strongly felt though sententious disclosure. When she would scold, she is more direct. Thus the rhetorical pattern of "Critics and Connoisseurs" is that of a series of assertions, each followed by an illustrative incident or a bit of evidence, the whole leading to the concluding edged question.

She indicates a liking for patterns in passages admiring the soaring of seagulls and pelican flocks, the careful craftsmanship of bottles and carriages. Her fondness for paradox suggests faith in an underlying order despite apparent incongruities; her customary linking, within a poem, of materials drawn from a diversity of sources strengthens the impression that one of her aims is to discover and to present a unity within multiplicity.

This belief helps account for incongruities of structure and wording, and these in turn allow her to express the paradoxes of existence. Her ability deftly to relate bric-a-brac enables her to come at a point from several angles and to avoid crude one-to-one comparisons. Though this probing of diversities often causes her to make abrupt juxtapositions and sudden shifts in syntax, she is careful not to let brilliance of individual lines overpower the poem. Indeed, just as she selects the conversational for use in quotations, so she avoids the trenchant aphorism in her own wording. Her wit is to inform the whole poem, not to give sparkle to individual lines.

Her frequent presentation of a long line followed by a shorter one could be used for the quick shifts in thought characteristic in poetry of wit, but she deliberately mutes her statement. The line patterns do allow surprises, but these are typically caused by her associations of seemingly disparate objects and insights, not by crisp or clever twists in argument. Disruptive clause placements serve to quicken the pace and to suggest intellectual meditation as well as to enable presentation of paradox.

Though some critics, notably Elizabeth Bishop, have cited various delights of metaphor, Miss Moore's work is almost peculiarly resistant to illustration by means of brief quotations. The metaphors and imagery are often not ones that will give the reader an immediate sense impression but ones that he must think through; her confidence is that, by thus inducing the reader to follow her thought, she can make her point more firmly than she could by use of the immediately sensational.

Restraint in style causes her frequently to omit connectives and to proceed from phase to phase of a poem by juxtaposition rather than by obvious transition. This method forces the reader to stretch his imagination—surely not an unhealthy form of exercise—and it rarely results in crypticism. If her associative processes are sometimes hard to follow, rereading generally proves that the fault has been lack of sufficient flexibility on the part of the reader. She is never cryptic because of private symbolism or merely fashionable metaphor; in "Picking and Choosing" she reproaches the critic who, "daft about the meaning," is fond of finding electric profundities in every simple candle. Restraint, she says in *Predilections*, extends even to this: the poet "ventures," he "commits" himself, and he has a right to expect the reader "to be able to complete poetic statement."

Miss Moore's diction is usually unobtrusive, the "good" colloquial English suited to the generally meditative and conversational tone of her poems. Occasionally, as in "To a Steam Roller," she will use Latinate vocabulary for philosophical reflections and short words for physical description. A full study of her diction, however, would disclose not a special poetic vocabulary but an interaction of ordinary words designed to exploit connotations and to encourage expression of paradox.

She does not always use rhyme, but when she does, it is subdued and intricate. It is very often unstressed, and, as with her wit and metaphor, she will go to some lengths to assure that it does not overpower her argument. She maintains restraint not only by the "feminine" rhyming of unstressed syllables but also by careful placing of words and phrases so that the word which ends in an unstressed rhyme is itself in a de-emphasized position. Her early work was famous for occasional breaking of words in the middle so that the first syllable of a word might end a line and serve as a rhyme to the eye, though not to the ear unless the reader chose to give it an unusual stress. She has often, but not always, revised her work in later printings so as to avoid these unusual rhymes; the continued presence of some of them in her most recent work demonstrates that she has come to use fewer of them not because she has developed an objection to the principle, but because she feels that in their unusualness they may obtrude and thus violate the governing principle of restraint.

Occasionally she will alter her handling of rhyme to create a special effect, as in "To a Steam Roller" where rather more emphatic rhyme than usual seems intended to suggest the solidity of the subject. Her willingness to experiment with rhyme is partly a device to make possible her use of highly disciplined metric.

Most of the time her line lengths are determined not by accentual-syllabic principles of conventional English metrics but by adhering to a precise syllable count, with the lines of one stanza parallel in length to the corresponding lines of the next one. Though French and Italian predecessors have been suggested for this custom, it seems more likely that Miss Moore acquired it from the experimentalism of American verse in the pre-World War I years. Adelaide Crapsey, Mina Loy, and other women poets of that era wrote poems in syllabic verse, and many "new" poets experimented with rigorously controlled

Japanese verse forms. Miss Moore herself gives great importance to matters of verse technique; her expertise in it was one of the qualities T. S. Eliot found of high value in his introduction to her *Selected Poems*. For the general reader, her meticulous counting of syllables, her careful parallelism of line lengths, and her intricate use of rhyme all reinforce her emphases upon discipline and precision.

Restraint appears in a variety of other ways. She seldom opens a poem with a resounding declaration or with a startlingly vivid figure; she prefers an artfully casual beginning in order to maintain her conversational tone. She sometimes ends a poem with a statement cast as a negative, a device she apparently hopes will avoid flatness that might arise from direct, prose-like assertion. In her revisions she has frequently sought to remove what seemed to her too obvious statements or intimations of prose-like "meaning." For example, she cut from "The Buffalo" a passage making it obvious that she was writing of a print, and she deleted from the *Collected Poems* printing of "Nine Nectarines" words in the original title that made it apparent she was dealing with the illustration on a piece of porcelain (her mind was not made up; she restored the words in *A Marianne Moore Reader*).

Miss Moore's use of notes and of quotations is also evidence of desire for discipline in assertion. As with Shelley's comments on "Queen Mab" and Eliot's notes to "The Waste Land," her notes often are not strictly necessary to an understanding of the poem. She is aware of this, and in *What Are Years* and—with slightly altered wording—in *Collected Poems* she included "A Note on the Notes" suggesting that the reader who finds the notes obtrusive might "take probity on faith" and disregard them. They do demonstrate her desire to give credit to sources, but of more importance is their function as evidence. They remind one of Hawthorne's device for persuading his reader that his stories were true, his habit of remarking that events he told of really did happen. Miss Moore has a similar desire to be taken as a truth-teller; hence her presentation of notes that, though unnecessary for anyone but the pedant, give an air of veracity. The notes to "Camellia Sabina," for example, are of interest in themselves but are scarcely enlightening for the reader of the poem; their function is demonstration that the odd and colorful materials are not merely imagined.

We scarcely need to know that the cat in "Peter" is the pet

of two friends, but a note to tell us this helps verify what is apparent in the poem: this is a particular cat, not a representative of some general quality of catness. It adds to our comprehension of "O to Be a Dragon!" to know which of various possible symbolisms Miss Moore has particular reference to, though even this poem is understandable without the citation. Sometimes her desire for precision causes her to let allusiveness become excessive: "Hometown Piece for Messrs. Alston and Reese," for example, is accessible only to the baseball fan or to the devoted reader willing to track down performances of now retired players in forgotten games. She has not always revised her notes when revising a poem; thus, some of the notes to "The Frigate Pelican" and to "An Octopus," retained in *Collected Poems*, apply only to passages deleted from that printing.

The quotations with which she fills her poems come from a multiplicity of sources: books of all sorts, newspapers, magazines, and, rarely, from speeches or conversations. She has sometimes explained her use of quotations as simply a convenience, asking, as in the foreword to *A Marianne Moore Reader*, "When a thing has been said so well that it could not be said better, why paraphrase it?" It makes her writing, she says, "a kind of collection of flies in amber." Actually her quotations are carefully selected to avoid the impression of a catalog of beauties; she quotes not the colorful or the aphoristic but the casual, not particularly artful remark that will contribute to the conversational tone she prefers. She also explains, in "A Note on the Notes," that her "hybrid method of composition" makes it ethically necessary for her to cite sources for her quotations and, in *A Marianne Moore Reader*, she has cited George Saintsbury as authority for the idea that direct quotation is the best method of exhibiting a personality.

The reader will notice that Miss Moore, being an artist rather than a scholar, freely alters quotations to make them fit her syntax or ideas. He will also notice that she by no means always cites a source for a quotation. Thus in "Poetry" she gives William Butler Yeats as the source for her famous phrasing "literalists of the imagination," but the exact wording is her own; recent printings put in quotation marks the poem's equally famous expression "imaginary gardens with real toads in them," but give no source for it. These considerations lead the reader to suspect that Miss Moore often uses quotation marks as a device of rhetoric rather than as an indication of borrowing.

Thus in the poem "Silence" she intends to keep herself at a slight remove from the material: putting most of the poem in quotation marks, as the *Collected Poems* printing does, enables her to present an assertive editorial commentary without seeming merely didactic. In *A Marianne Moore Reader* she achieves the same result though putting only two lines in quotation marks, because she so handles the material as to make most of the rest of the lines seem an indirect quotation. Together with the fact that she alters the wording of the quotation she cites as her source for the idea of the poem, these usages indicate that not scholarly accuracy but artistic presentation governs her use of quotation marks. Both notes and quotations are sometimes means of giving credit to sources; but more often they seem intended to subdue any impression of assertiveness, to suggest that responsibility for a bit of lore or a remark does not lie directly on the poet.

Another device for maintaining restraint in commentary is use of animals as subjects. Miss Moore knows not only that we will recognize qualities and behaviors in animals akin to those of our human associates, but also that our awareness that a matter after all concerns "lower" creatures will enable us to save face while absorbing the lesson. Her use of an animal differs markedly from that of the fabulist, for though she presents her animal in action, she seldom involves it in a narrative. Moreover, she consistently uses animals to represent desirable qualities; it is man who is guilty of greed, falseness, misuse, and other errors she condemns. She does not commit a pathetic fallacy: because of her objectivism, her jerboa and pangolin and basilisk are clearly themselves, not men in little.

Her ideas on the relationship of man and animals are most fully illustrated in "The Pangolin," a poem showing that man, though he may draw lessons from animal behavior, has other and profounder responsibilities. She frequently writes of exotic animals, partly to take advantage of the color and excitement of the unusual, but also to avoid stock associations—she does not want to weaken her presentation by relying on faithful dogs, sly foxes, and innocent sheep. The animal world, in addition, gives her a handy set of references, something the twentieth-century poet, unable to depend upon familiarity with classic myth or even with biblical allusions, often feels compelled to get along without. The exotic nature of some of her creatures is not a bar to communication, since it is easy to give a sufficient description. As we might expect, the animals she most often writes of are the self-sufficient who survive by disciplined behavior. She wrote in the foreword to *A Marianne Moore Reader* that the animal is an exemplar of art because of his naturalness. His self-discipline provides a useful lesson for errant man.

She has her idiosyncrasies. Like her contemporary, the impressionist writer Van Wyck Brooks, she frequently uses British spellings (in later printings she has sometimes changed to American forms). She has occasionally experimented with punctuation marks, especially with colons and semicolons in "The Labours of Hercules" and "England"; her usages do not seem consistent. She changes from single to double quotation marks at nearly every printing, her preference perhaps depending upon the appearance of the marks in particular type faces. She sometimes uses as a title the first line of a poem; since this would cause the reader to read the words twice, she often leaves the title in the usual large type but counts it as the first line, so that what seems at first glance to be the opening line is actually the second. Her titles sometimes are functional in other respects as well. Only the title of "Sun" makes it explicit that the sun is the object addressed in the poem; and one might have difficulty recognizing that refugees are the subject of "Rescue with Yul Brynner" were it not for the title's hint.

III   *A Kind of Tame Excitement*

Devotion to her poetic career—as well, perhaps, as desire for the armoring which "silence" affords—has kept Miss Moore thus far from writing an autobiography. The idea has occurred to her, of course. Pascal Covici of Viking Press assured her, she told me, that she would have to work only an hour and a half a day to produce an autobiography.[3] But, she remarked, she cannot work "that way": she thinks always of whatever work she has in hand at the moment and prefers not to take on more than one task at a time. She has been courteous to interviewers, has supplied brief write-ups for biographical guidebooks, and has published a few essays touching on aspects of her biography.

She says that if her life story is written it will be a "very tame affair." It will be that if the biographer concentrates on the routine dates and dimensions of her life. Thousands of women have taught school and worked in a library, and many of them have lived the scarcely munificent life of a free-lance poet. Even editorship of *The Dial,* outstanding though Miss Moore's conduct of it was, was hardly in itself a flamboyantly unusual activity for an American writer in the 1920's. An understanding of her talents must come from somewhere other than a résumé of her outward circumstances.

Miss Moore was born in Kirkwood, Missouri, a suburb of St. Louis, on November 15, 1887, the second child of Mary and John Milton Moore. Her father, an engineer, had just suffered a nervous breakdown after failure of his plans to manufacture a smokeless furnace and had gone home to his parents in Portsmouth, Ohio. Mrs. Moore had consequently returned to the home of her father, the Reverend John Riddle Warner, a Scotch-Irish Presbyterian minister. Though the Reverend Warner met the Reverend Eliot at St. Louis clerical functions, the families of Miss Moore and of T. S. Eliot, who was born in St. Louis ten months after Miss Moore, were not socially acquainted.

Mrs. Moore remained in Kirkwood as her father's housekeeper until he died in 1894. She then took her two children—John was seventeen months older than Marianne—to Carlisle, Pennsylvania, where she lived on a small inheritance. For a time she was an English teacher at Carlisle's Metzger Institute, a school for girls that has since become a part of Dickinson College. The attachment of the three Moores to each other remained close. Mrs. Moore lived with Marianne until her death in 1947, and Miss Moore, who dedicated *Collected Poems* to her, still respects her mother's precision in language (she reports herself somewhat irritated, for example, by a reporter's misquotation that had her mother end a sentence with "around"). Her brother John made a career as a navy chaplain; upon retiring from the service he became chaplain at the Gunnery School, a preparatory institution for boys in Washington, Connecticut. Though in 1962 he had retired from that position, he was still spending much time on school affairs—too much, in the opinion of Miss Moore.

Miss Moore attended the Metzger schools and entered Bryn Mawr College in Bryn Mawr, Pennsylvania, in 1905. There is perhaps exaggeration in her remark to *Current Biography* that she spent most of her time in the biology laboratory because she was too "immature" for the English and language courses she was interested in; she did publish a number of poems in the college literary magazines. One fellow student was Hilda

Doolittle ("H.D."), who was later to help publish Miss Moore's first book. After graduating with a Bachelor of Arts degree in 1909, Miss Moore took a secretarial course at Carlisle Commercial College; and, for three and a half years from 1911 to 1915, she taught stenography, typing, bookkeeping, commercial English, and commercial law at the United States Indian School in Carlisle. These subjects did not inspire her, she later told a *New Yorker* reporter; she would have preferred to stay home and read. Write-ups remark on the point that Jim Thorpe, the famous Indian athlete, took courses from her; always an admirer of the skilled and graceful, she told a *Newsweek* reporter that Thorpe was chivalrous and kind. As for herself, she says she was a poor teacher.

Meanwhile, her brother John, after graduating from Yale, had been ordained a Presbyterian minister, and in 1916 was appointed pastor at the Ogden Memorial Church in Chatham, New Jersey, where Miss Moore with her mother moved to keep house for him. But when America entered World War I, John joined the Navy and Marianne with her mother rented a basement apartment in Greenwich Village where they lived for eleven years.

In these second and third decades of the century Miss Moore won recognition rather quickly as one of the leading spirits in the "new" poetry and, both because of her own creative work and because of her position on *The Dial*, became one of the best known literary writers in America. Her professional publication began in 1915 when *The Egoist*, a London journal specializing in Imagist verse, printed her "To the Soul of 'Progress'" (later "To Military Progress"). Miss Moore was not an Imagist, whatever that term may mean; she was of course acquainted with H.D., who had married Richard Aldington, writer and editor of the magazine. A month later, in May, 1915, *Poetry* magazine published five of Miss Moore's poems. Since Harriet Monroe, its founding editor, had made *Poetry* the leading journal for the new generation of American poets, this publication meant that Miss Moore was recognized as one of the innovators.

Through the World War I period and the early 1920's Miss Moore's poems were printed in a variety of the "little" magazines which during these years appeared and disappeared with a rapidity paced to the uncertainties of their amateur publishers' checking accounts. One prominent little magazine enterpriser was Alfred Kreymborg, himself a poet, who associated with many of the "new" poets then working in the New York area, among them William Carlos Williams, Kenneth Burke, Wallace Stevens, Conrad Aiken, John Gould Fletcher, Richard Aldington, Mina Loy, and Miss Moore. In *Troubador,* his autobiographical account of these years, Kreymborg reported that many of the group admired Miss Moore—for her flaming red hair and her "mellifluous flow of polysyllables which held every man in awe" as well as for her poetry. He also said that John Marshall, a partner in New York's The Little Bookshop Around the Corner, intended not long after 1915 to publish volumes of poetry by a number of the new writers, including Miss Moore as well as Williams, Stevens, Maxwell Bodenheim, Skip Cannell, and Kreymborg himself. One or more poems by Miss Moore appeared in each of Kreymborg's annual *Others* anthologies of new verse for the years 1916, 1917, and 1919.

Ezra Pound's early recognition of Miss Moore's talents is indicated in his published letters. He wrote to Miss Monroe in May, 1915, praising Miss Moore's titles; and by 1918 he was remarking that Miss Moore, together with Williams and Mina Loy, was a central figure in discussion of poetry. Williams too was an early friend. Though in his *Autobiography* he speculates that he may have "brushed against" Miss Moore when he visited girls at Bryn Mawr, his association with her appears to have begun when he helped Kreymborg edit the journal *Others.* Frequent references to her in the *Autobiography* and in his *Selected Letters* indicate that he and Miss Moore shared in their group's feeling that they were engaged in an important cultural enterprise. Like Kreymborg, Williams speaks of Miss Moore's red hair, imaginative conversation, and effect of innocence. "Marianne was our saint," he wrote. "Everyone loved her." Williams' letters also demonstrate his professional respect for her; they show him asking her advice and commenting upon her opinions with the seriousness of a fellow craftsman.

After moving to New York, Miss Moore worked for a time as a tutor. But she frequented the Hudson Park branch of the New York Public Library, where in 1921 she was given a part time job as an assistant at a salary of $50.00 a month. She told a *Newsweek* reporter in 1951 that she was not much of an asset there because she could never find anything; as with her derogation of her own teaching at Carlisle, this comment is possibly more accurate as an indication of modesty than as a report of fact. Her first book publication came in 1921. Without Miss Moore's knowledge, Winifred Ellerman (known under the pen-name Bryher), then the wife of Robert McAlmon, and H.D., both of whom had been associated with the Imagists, had *Poems* brought out under the imprint of The Egoist Press. A note in Miss Moore's second book, *Observations* (1924), says that the *Poems* "collection" was "made and arranged by H.D. and Mr. and Mrs. Robert McAlmon." This statement was later reported in *Twentieth Century Authors;* in the supplement to that publication, Miss Moore said that the work was the effort of Bryher and H.D., Robert McAlmon not being involved. All twenty-four of the works in *Poems* had appeared in magazines.

Into the early 1920's, Miss Moore had a high reputation within the avant-garde but no fame among the broader group of Americans with cultural interests. Wide recognition came through her association with *The Dial*. This journal had been "re-established," as Miss Moore puts it in a retrospective *Partisan Review* essay, in New York in 1920 after a varied, often distinguished career in Chicago and a short tenure under other management in New York. Now it was taken over by two well-to-do backers, Scofield Thayer and Dr. J. S. Watson, who sought to print what an announcement in the June, 1925, issue called "works of merit not welcomed by commercial magazines."

Abandoning the social emphasis of the magazine's former pub-lishers, they turned it into a periodical of the arts that functioned through the 1920's as the most vigorous, most highly regarded of American journals of culture. It was renowned not only for its literature but also for its commentary on music, drama, and fine arts, and for its photographs of paintings and sculpture. Its international luster is indicated by a sampling of its con-tributors. The November, 1924, issue, for example, had contri-butions from Miss Moore ("Sea Unicorns and Land Unicorns"), Kenneth Burke, Marc Chagall (a color photograph of a paint-ing), Oswald Spengler, James Stephens, Jules Romains, Thomas Mann, and Edmund Wilson. Miss Moore was the first of her group to win publication in *The Dial*. According to Kreymborg, Miss Moore was asked to submit her work after she read her poem "England" at a party one night in 1920. *The Dial*, though "little" enough compared with the mass circulation magazines, was already much better known and more stable than most literary periodicals; appearance in it gave Miss Moore a sizable audience. From then on, her work appeared in it frequently.

Direct association with *The Dial* followed publication of Miss Moore's second book, her first to appear in this country. By 1924 Williams was writing from Paris to report that Robert McAlmon wanted to publish a book of her work; Williams himself wanted to write a preface for it. *Observations* appeared in late 1924, however, as a publication of the Dial Press without direct aid from Williams. It incorporated all but three of the pieces earlier published in *Poems* and added several others. Its title was meant to suggest that the contents were both perceptions and commentaries; it made use of what was at the time a fashionable word (for example, T. S. Eliot's first book title: *Prufrock and Other Observations*).

This book was a milestone in Miss Moore's public career, winning recognition that would be surpassed only by that given *Collected Poems. The Dial's* founders had established a cash award of two thousand dollars (not a "prize," as Miss Moore explains in her essay on the magazine) for achievement in poetry; the first award had been made to Eliot in 1922. The award for 1924 was given to Miss Moore. It was doubtless welcome for its cash as well as for its recognition. Pound's letters during the early 1920's suggested raising money to enable American poets, including Miss Moore, to spend time in Europe; they also suggested her to the Guggenheim Foundation for an award. Poetry is not in our century a money-making endeavor.

The award led in turn to an *annus mirabilis* in the pages of *The Dial,* for five consecutive issues now carried tributes to her work. Glenway Wescott opened the parade with a general article in the January, 1925, issue; the unsigned "Comment" columns of February, March, and April praised her; and Williams reviewed *Observations* in May. This accumulated recognition, together with the journal's frequent publication of her poems and reviews, made it scarcely surprising to readers of the June "Announcement" that, upon the resignation of Alyse Gregory as managing editor and the decision of Scofield Thayer himself to withdraw from active editing, Miss Moore was appointed acting editor beginning with the July, 1925, issue. The statement explained that Miss Moore would actively assist Dr. Watson in choosing the contents of the magazine, and would exercise the publication chores until now performed by the managing editor; Thayer himself and Dr. Watson were to continue to appoint the magazine's correspondents, select the Dial Award recipient, and choose the frontispiece. A year later, however, the June, 1926, issue announced that Thayer was resigning and that Miss Moore had been named editor. From this point until appearance of the final issue in July, 1929, Miss Moore was actively engaged in the day-to-day editing, correspondence, and publication details of the nation's most prominent journal of arts.

Proof of her success is the continued high reputation of the magazine, testified to by such diverse commentators as Frederick Hoffman ("the editorial sensibility of the decade," he wrote of her in *The Twenties*), E. E. Cummings (lack of greater recognition of the periodical is owing to a "conspiracy" of "intellectual gangsters," he said in *Six Nonlectures*), and *Newsweek* (the journal fixed most presently established literary reputations, it said in 1951).

There were, of course, some private and public detractors. Gorham B. Munson in *Destinations* accused Miss Moore of lacking "impartial free intelligence," and she herself told Donald Hall in an interview (in *A Marianne Moore Reader*) of Hart Crane's quarrels with her editing. Others thought *The Dial* rather guarded than advanced. Bernard Smith, a Marxist, in his *Forces in American Criticism* found it, as might be expected, too "esthetic." The *New Republic* in 1927 made the astounding accusation that *The Dial* had not introduced a single new American writer of interest (an unsigned "Comment" column in *The Dial* gave the deft reply that the interest was in writing, not in writers). Even Williams, though exempting Miss Moore from his condemnation, by 1928 was writing in letters that he was "disgusted" with what he thought were the magazine's "half-hearted ways" and "worthlessness"; since he did not specify his dislikes, we may assume that it no longer was novel enough for him.

Important as was her contribution to American letters as *The Dial's* editor, Miss Moore's real career was in poetry. But she had little time for writing while editing the magazine: the New York Public Library bibliography of her work lists no verse from 1925 to 1932. When, in 1929, Dr. Watson gave up his interest to return to his home in Rochester, New York, Miss Moore alone of the magazine's chief spirits remained. The announcement of the end of publication was an abrupt note at the end of the July issue, initialed by Dr. Watson. Since then Miss Moore has done no professional editing (though in 1931 and 1932 Ezra Pound strongly urged grooming her to succeed Harriet Monroe as editor of *Poetry*). Her essay on *The Dial* is in a vein of celebratory, nostalgic reminiscence, kept from false sentiment by freshness of perception.

The change in her public career was matched by one perhaps equally important in her private life. Her mother had become ill, and her brother John was stationed at the Brooklyn Navy Yard. It seemed convenient for the women to move from their Greenwich Village basement apartment to Brooklyn's Cumberland Street and into the fifth-floor apartment where Miss Moore still lives. Here she has spent an active three decades as free-lance poet, book reviewer, and article writer, continuing upon occasion to serve the cause of new poetry.

After the hiatus of the years on *The Dial,* she resumed publication of her verse. By 1934, a decade had passed since she had last put together a book. Apparently her friends were urging her to publish one; Elizabeth Sergeant reports (in *Robert Frost: The Trial by Existence*) that Frost was one of those offering to help. But arrangements were already being made for *Selected Poems,* which was brought out in 1935 by Macmillan in America and by Faber and Faber in England. This volume reprinted, often with alterations, most of the pieces published in *Poems* and *Observations,* and a number of others from magazines. Adoption by a commercial publisher gave the work relatively wide distribution, the new was no longer shocking, *The Dial* had given her an established reputation, and the book had an introduction by Eliot; for all these reasons, *Selected Poems* became primary in considerations of her work.

She published short books at intervals over the next fifteen years. *The Pangolin and Other Verse* (1936) printed five poems; some of these were among the fifteen published in 1941 under the title *What Are Years.* Six more appeared in *Nevertheless* (1944); and the poem "A Face" was published separately in 1949. She brought these publications together in *Collected Poems* (1951). Her translation of La Fontaine's *Fables,* begun in the mid-1940's, was published in 1954. She continued to win prizes—the Shelley Memorial Award in 1940, the Contemporary Poetry's Patrons' Prize and the Harriet Monroe Poetry Award in 1944, a Guggenheim Fellowship in 1945, and a joint grant from the American Academy of Arts and Letters and the National Institute of Arts and Letters in 1946. She taught composition at Cummington School, Massachusetts, in 1942, beginning a career as an occasional academician that has since taken her to poetry seminars, reading sessions, and lectureships at such schools as

Bryn Mawr, Vassar, California (both in Berkeley and in Los Angeles), and Harvard. In 1949 she received the first of what was to become a long string of honorary degrees, a Litterarum Doctor from Wilson College.

Publication of *Collected Poems* brought her a second *annus mirabilis*—the Pulitzer Prize, the National Book Award, and the Bollingen Prize. This work even established Miss Moore as something of a celebrity. Her fame is indicated by a *New Yorker* magazine interview that makes much of her status as a Brooklynite, a *Newsweek* article illustrated with a small picture of her and a large one of Jim Thorpe, and the ultimate accolade of "*Life* Goes on a Zoo Tour with a Famous Poet." Small wonder that in 1955 and 1956, when Ford Motor Company was *enceinte* with a new model, it called upon Miss Moore to suggest a name. Could the quick failure of the venture be punishment for the company's decision to use, instead of one of Miss Moore's suggestions, the family appellation Edsel? In the later 1950's and the 1960's, Miss Moore's work was appearing even in such magazines as *Vogue* and *Harper's Bazaar*, doubtless puzzling those who stumbled across it while thumbing through the fashion advertisements. Meanwhile, she brought out *Gedichte* (1954), a bilingual choice of her work; *Selected Fables* (1955); *Predilections* (1955), a selection of her essays and reviews; new poems in *Like a Bulwark* (1956) and *O to Be a Dragon* (1959); *A Marianne Moore Reader* (1961), a miscellany of poems and prose; and *The Absentee* (1962), a dramatized retelling of Maria Edgeworth's prose story. She continued to publish verse in magazines, and also prepared for publication in 1963 a version of three Charles Perrault fairy tales.

Amidst all this she remained an active citizen of Brooklyn She has written proudly of her city's advantages for the imag· inatively curious; she says in her essay "Brooklyn from Clinton Hill" that it has afforded her "the kind of tame excitement on which I thrive." Her neighborhood today is typical of miles of Brooklyn residential areas. Its streets are lined with old three-story, red brick homes, many of them now housing two families. The population is mixed Negro, Puerto Rican, and "Caucasian." Most of the houses are built wall to wall and close to the side-walk, so that the yard area is only a patch of perhaps five feet by ten. In some cases there is grass in this patch; at least as often, it is bare dirt with a garbage can or two and perhaps a tethered dog. On a sunny spring afternoon the streets are busy

[38]

with playing children, strolling dog-walkers, and honking auto-
mobiles; house-dressed women idle in their windows, calling to
each other or watching the life of the sidewalks. Though poor
by the standards of suburbia, the neighborhood is not what
New Yorkers would consider a slum. It offers an active, colorful
multiplicity that is doubtless attractive to a poet whose real
occupation has been observation.

Miss Moore's own home is an apartment in a once yellow,
now gray stone building, narrow enough and, at five stories,
low enough to be inconspicuous behind the trees whose leaves
shade it in the summer. It has a touch of oldtime elegance in
the two "mothballs" or white globes set on low black stands on
either side of the front door. Miss Moore lives on the top floor.
Entering her apartment, one passes down a longish hallway
lined with shelves of books and bric-a-brac (including a foot-
square picture of a porcupine). The hall goes past her bedroom,
where a dresser and shelves hold manila envelopes of correspondence and the wall decorations include pictures of classic
scenes like those that used to illustrate high-school Latin books.
The living room—dining room areas continue the impression of a
place for comfortable living, not at all stylish or modern. At one
end of the living room is a large table on which sits an old
clock with a floral front; there are two or three comfortable
chairs, a variety of end tables, books on shelves and tables.
There is a view of trees and streets, though a black iron fire
escape edges down outside one window. The setting is neither
sentimentally homey nor fashionably uncomfortable. It has the
look of the well-worn and in work areas is efficient but not fussy.

Miss Moore meets her visitor at the door with a firm hand-
shake and asks if he found the elevator, a question she will come
back to, as she has been distressed by the sight of friends
puffing their way up the stairs. She is a slender, blue-eyed
woman of medium height who puts on glasses to read and wears
her hair, now gray to white, looped in a long coil around the
top of her head. She seats her guest, serves orange juice and
crackers, and, when she first sits down, seems to withdraw
slightly as if to brace herself for an ordeal. But in conversation
she becomes animated, and moves from topic to topic in a series
of juxtapositions reminiscent of the technique of her poetry.
In one three- or four-minute passage she can move from praise
of a scholar in English from Belgrade to commendation of a
dramatic version of E. M. Forster's *A Passage to India,* then to

her enjoyment of a lecture by Thornton Wilder, and to favorable remarks about Theodore Roethke's teaching in Seattle; on to praise of Karl Barth; and finally to mention of criticism of her writing at Bryn Mawr (an instructor told her she hid her point in writing; but, she says, "I survived it."). All this she knits together, in this instance the theme being the need for clearness in expression.

She will give anecdotes of other writers, but swears her auditor not to relay unfavorable ones because she "will not denigrate" anyone in public. She talks of the need to spend her morning hours keeping up with correspondence and, somewhat sadly, of the fact that people ask her for photographs. Some readers, one gathers, have been spoiled in their expectations by accounts of motion picture celebrities who have studio publicity budgets; they make demands which are excessive upon the energies and funds of a poet who has neither private wealth nor extensive commercial support. In her attempts to be helpful, she reports, she has stumbled "into all kinds of predicaments." She adds: "I am not suspicious; I do not hate people; I do get taken in quite often."

Certainly in her reception of a visitor Miss Moore is solicitous and helpful. She shows a passage from a work in progress, exhibits proofs of a poem about to be printed, checks on the level of orange juice in the glass, apologizes for a smell of floor cleaner in the hallway (though praising the janitress for her effort), and urgently reminds the departing guest of the elevator. A visit with her is an experience anyone would hurry to repeat if it were not for the reflection that she already meets too many demands on her time and courtesies.

CHAPTER 2

The Armored Self:
Selected Poems

M ISS MOORE'S strategies and emphases change, but there is a consistency throughout her work. She believes that behavior and esthetic practice should follow the same principles and that both should be based on a perception of "rock crystal" reality. This reality shows that man's world is one whose multiple appearances must be recognized but must not be allowed to obscure the unity of spirit and matter. Her poetry is a continual meditation upon this point and upon the consequent necessities in human behavior. Men live in an environment containing both comfort and peril; the ideal for human performance is heroism. The characteristics of heroism include ability to perceive reality, genuineness, courage, and self-discipline without coldness and without sternness. Man must be aware of mystery but not therefore be esoteric; he must admit complexity but retain clarity and spontaneity; he must value restraint and art but not thereby lose ardor. These and related principles are her topics throughout her career. Because differences in method and approach do develop, one may conveniently divide her work into periods, with the first of these culminating in *Selected Poems*.

I *Rock Crystal Things to See*

Selected Poems (1935) incorporates—frequently with minor alterations and sometimes with major revisions—most of the works published in *Poems* (1921) and *Observations* (1924) and most of her other verse of the 1920's and early 1930's. With some further revisions, the 1935 volume is reprinted as the opening section of *Collected Poems* (1951). Since the latter represents the latest version of most of its contents, it is the best basis for discussion.

The opening two poems are portions of a piece originally printed in 1932 with three sections under the general heading "Part of a Novel, Part of a Poem, Part of a Play"; three individual sections were headed "The Steeple-Jack," "The Student," and "The Hero." Of these, "The Student" was reprinted only in *What Are Years* (1941). "The Hero" and a shortened version of "The Steeple-Jack" appeared in *Selected Poems*. "The Steeple-Jack," with the dropped lines restored and with several alterations in wording, appeared again in *A Marianne Moore Reader* (1961).

The "confusion" that exists in the seemingly placid environment of an ordinary town is examined in "The Steeple-Jack." The town, which represents the environment of most human lives, is calm, seemingly well ordered. Yet we remember that to be human is to face death—an inevitability Miss Moore neither grows lyrical over like Whitman nor rages against like Dylan Thomas but accepts as part of reality. The first four stanzas, which picture the setting, open with the remark that the scene would have appealed to Albrecht Dürer, the German Renaissance artist. The reader is to recognize that Dürer is famed for placing apocalyptic visions in everyday settings. The poem presents the town on a "fine day" when there are "formal" waves on the water, an orderly flock of seagulls lazily circling the spires, water changing color in definite bands, and fishermen who have carefully spread their nets for drying. Yet this scene is not entirely tidy: on the beach there are eight stranded whales (mention of an exact number adds to the impression of precision); the gulls, though steady, nevertheless quiver slightly; and, we are reminded, when storms come they put in disarray both grass and stars. (We may also recall that in one of her best-known poems, "A Grave," Miss Moore has the sea function as a deceptive peril to man.) The words of the fourth stanza, "it is a privilege to see so/much confusion," sum up the appearance of the scene and the poet's attitude that a view of it is revelatory.

The last four stanzas present a specific example of the "confusion" noted in the town's general aspect and find a unity in the apparent variety. A steeplejack in red, the color of warning, leaves a danger sign on the sidewalk while he gilds the star on a church spire. This little scene in itself constitutes one of the paradoxes of which Miss Moore is fond. She delights in such discoveries because they apparently please her in themselves and because they seem to signify qualities inextricable from experience. She is most sure that she is presenting the nature of things not when she can give a clear—a simplified— explanation but when she can illustrate discontinuities. Belief in oneness must not deny diversities.

Quick statement of other details of the scene concludes that here the hero, the student, and the steeplejack, "each in his way,/ is at home." They are at home, we may assume, because this is a typical human community and these are types to be found among the "simple people" who live in it.

Yet perhaps these people are not merely simple. The last stanza opens with the seemingly casual, yet almost heavily ironic remark, "It scarcely could be dangerous to be living/in a town like this," among people who have a steeplejack place danger signs by a church while he gilds the steeple star that, the poet says, stands for hope. "Simple people" go about their business; they accept danger and hope as parts of life. Hope and danger, the poem seems to tell us, are inextricably mixed in life, are two primary qualities of it. This does not sadden the poet, for it is a "privilege" to see this mixture, the multitudinous and often paradoxical combinations of order and disorder, calm and storm, faith and doubt which make up our environment; it is exhilarating, her tone tells us. The attitude is that life is a mixture of possibilities that we would do well to face with an optimism that may be more than faint though it must be sensibly restrained.

Cuts from the *Collected Poems* version eliminated four whole stanzas and portions of two others. Perhaps at the time Miss Moore felt that the lines prettified the scene or heaped on unnecessary detail. The cutting, however, shortened the fourth stanza, slightly marring the neatness of the poem's finish. And it was criticized by Randall Jarrell because it omitted several lines on a "college student/named Ambrose" who is still mentioned in the seventh stanza. Jarrell's objection seems unnecessary, for in the *Collected Poems* printing the student is simply one of a list of types to be found in the town; neither a name for him nor a characterization of him is required.

Whether because of these or other considerations, the longer version is given in *A Marianne Moore Reader.* The effect of the restored descriptive passages in this version is to make the scene itself and the student Ambrose serve as further instances of the paradoxes the poem is presenting. The lines detail the scene's mixture of northern and semitropical flora, the town apparently being one in a northern area warmed by an ocean current; the passage on the student remarks that he has a "not-native" hat and books, yet he likes the "elegance" which is native to the place.

Given such conditions for life, the ideal person is the "hero," the title figure of the second poem surviving from what was a set of three. Its six stanzas describe the hero as the man who perceives "the rock/crystal thing to see," who retains hope though ground for it has vanished, and who is tolerant of others' errors. The first three stanzas show that the hero is representative; like the rest of us, he has certain dislikes and fears; he vexes some men and is vexed by others. In detailing these aspects of the hero Miss Moore writes with a convincing verve: few are so insensitive that they too do not shrink when they read that, as any of us might do,

> . . . The hero shrinks
> As what it is flies out on muffled wings, with twin yellow
> eyes—to and fro—
>
> with quavering water-whistle note, low,
>   high, in basso-falsetto chirps
>   until the skin creeps.

As often in her writing, Miss Moore's method here has been to set down tersely general statements—that the hero does not like such requirements as "going where one does not wish/to go" and "suffering and not/saying so"—and then to give a vivid exemplification of the appropriate emotion.

Having woven a groundwork of specifics and illustration, Miss Moore in her last three stanzas moves on to commentary that is broader in scope though still conveyed by example and illustration. The hero in his hopefulness and tolerance is lenient toward human error even when its source is plain silliness. An instance is the behavior of a guide at Washington's tomb in Mount Vernon, Virginia, who maintains his decorum and his "reverence for mystery" despite the trivial questioning of a tourist "hobo" who uses her tongue instead of her eyes. The hero thus is true to his own nature. Moses, we are told, "would not be grandson to Pharaoh"; we are to recall that Moses, found and raised by Pharaoh's daughter, upon reaching adulthood left the Egyptians to lead the oppressed Hebrews whom he felt to be his own people. Yet the hero eats what is not his "natural meat": he does, it would seem, not what might give him pleasure but, like Moses, what his circumstances make it ethically necessary for him to do.

The concluding commentary, for which all that goes before has carefully prepared us, is that the hero sees reality. This is not a mere "sight" such as the woman at Washington's tomb was seeking, but "the rock/crystal thing to see." We deduce that this would be reality of experience and situation, including the nature of one's obligations. A second major quality is that the hero "covets" nothing that he has "let go." The hero desires none of the temptations he has dismissed: he has learned, and he confirms in his behavior, what truth is and what restraint he must show in confronting it. The nature of our environment as shown in "The Steeple-Jack" and the ideal of conduct as explained in "The Hero" are related. The hero recognizes paradox and, seeing it, does not evade it. Like the guide at the tomb and like Moses in Egypt, he has the self-discipline necessary under his circumstances. Seeing clearly, he does what he has to do. Clear sight includes a recognition of ethical responsibility, a responsibility that is as much a part of reality as mausoleum stone and desert sand.

The poem "The Student," which originally appeared with "The Steeple-Jack" and "The Hero," does not deal with the Ambrose mentioned in "The Steeple-Jack." This poem is a general consideration of the student as hero in a modified Emersonian sense; he is a man of quiet, spiritual courage. Its dominant purpose, however, is reflection upon American immaturity, shown by contrasting Americans with what the poem depicts as the wise French. Americans, it says, are all "undergraduates"; but the French, though not so enthusiastic for formal education, have managed to "grow up." The poem thus is not closely related to the others with which it originally appeared; it is to be compared rather with such commentary on national characteristics as "England."

The reality that the hero perceives is the topic of the next three poems. "The Jerboa" has two sections contrasting wasteful and artificial luxury with spare but genuine simplicity. The opening lines of "Too Much," the poem's first section, indicate that the picture the stanzas are to present will be unfavorable. A Roman, we are told, had his artist "contrive"—a word Miss Moore uses to imply falsity in execution—a fountain of indeterminate shape, somewhat like a pine cone or a fir cone. Since to Miss Moore precision is of high value, the point that the shape is imprecise suggests a serious fault. Looking like something suited for the luxuriant courts of ancient Egypt, this object has nevertheless passed for art.

The remaining sixteen stanzas of the section describe the waste and artificiality of the Pharaohs, citing their use of slaves, their lordly misuse of animals, their coy games. All their decorative art, the poem says, was delicately wrought or cleverly done—at a "fine distance" from such realities as drought. Miss Moore makes her point by building up a series of exact details, though in presenting these she makes her attitudes obvious. In Stanza eight, for example, she uses "toys" for such supposedly useful adult objects as toilet boxes and the royal totem. The strongest condemnation is in stanzas eleven and twelve, which remark that dwarfs, kept to lend an "evident"—too obvious—"poetry" to the court scene, gave it a "fantasy" and a "verisimilitude" that seem right in any age to "those with . . . power over the poor." The whole environment was grotesque, a distortion, even a perversion, of what life should be: the court of the Pharaohs was an enormous falsity built on the toil of workers who meant no more to their masters than a fancy cane or a clever folding bedroom. In pastoral-like court games, princes dressed as women, and women as men; the Pharaoh "gave his name" to images of serpents and beetles, and "was named for them"—he was, that is, like these lifeless parodies of reality.

The last stanzas mention Pharaoh's mongoose, kept to kill the very snakes whose images figured in court rites and games. The pampering of this creature suggests by contrast the natural-ness of the jerboa which had, we may assume, an entirely different and better kind of "happiness." Unlike the mongoose, which was "restless" under the fondling and restraint of its artificial existence, the jerboa had "rest" and "joy" in its desert setting, a home lacking the comforts of court life but providing necessities. "One"—anyone who perceives sensibly—would prefer the jerboa's life to that of the mongoose.

Mention of "plenty" in the last line of the first section leads to the second section, "Abundance." In it Miss Moore presents nine stanzas of delighted observation of the jerboa (the *Collected Poems* printing drops the original fourth stanza, a descriptive passage). She gives no overt moralizing, but the exhilaration with which she recounts the details suggests the creature's function as an example of one's living in awareness of himself and his surroundings. His adaptation does not give him a shallow reaction to his circumstances, for he is neither "well adjusted" nor gloomy, neither conservative nor progressive. Like a desert Thoreau, he is in this world to *live* in it.

"Africanus," the section begins, should have meant not the Roman conqueror who was spoken of reverently under that title, but those "untouched" by greed and pride: the free-born jerboa and the native "blacks" whose harmony with their surroundings is ignored by the supposed great men who are blinded by greed and pride. The man Jacob was led by a mirage to see a ladder to heaven; but the jerboa's perceptions are not mistaken. It can alternately rest and leap, it can hop like a chipmunk or launch itself into the air like a bird as occasion demands; it is "simplified" to efficiency. It is typical of Miss Moore's rigorous though wryly gentle perceptions that she sees the moon not as having sentimentally prettified the jerboa but as having "silvered" it to "steel." The moon and the jerboa both being in harmony with the place, the one strengthens the other.

The theme of harmony is continued through the seventh stanza, where the jerboa is pictured as "assuming" the color of the desert sands; that his paws folded close in to his torso seem of a piece with it rather than attachments to it also suggests a kind of physical wholeness to the creature himself. The last two stanzas make appropriate use of terms and images drawn from music to marvel at the jerboa's way of running; they say that his very footprints are like impressions of fern seed (a magical substance in Miss Moore's poem "Spenser's Ireland"). The closing lines suggest setting his leaps to music, admire the "Chippendale" artistry of his claw, and hint again at his wholeness by mentioning that his three-toed claw is matched by his resting posture on two feet and tail.

There is rigor of perception throughout the poem: a tail is a tail, not a plume or banner; a claw is a claw, not a pedestal. Yet the effect is not harsh, partly because possible severity is made rich by the counterpoint of rhythm. In the first section the pace is relatively slow and careful, as though Miss Moore wants to make sure that the scorn of her lines is understood. The formal metrics of the second section is the same as that of the first—there is the same number of syllables in parallel lines, the same number of lines in stanzas, the same rhyme scheme. But the section is faster in pace. This quickening

matches in its tripping effects the imagery drawn from musician-
ship; and it contributes to the celebratory tone Miss Moore
desires for her presentation of the creature which lives not in a
surfeit of artificial "plenty" but in that genuine harmony with
his surroundings which to the poet constitutes true "abundance."

The next two poems also ponder the contrast between the
merely luxuriant, the artificial or spurious, and the natural, the
genuine which, though it may be beautiful, is also useful.
"Camellia Sabina" contrasts the pampered flower of that name
and the carefully tended grape used for wine making with the
equally cared for food-grape, and of course says the latter is
preferable. Using a relatively long line, Miss Moore gives the
poem a slow pace, a tone that is reflective though wry.
The intention is that we are to take it seriously but not grimly.
What are in *Collected Poems* the last four lines of each stanza
were printed as three lines in *Selected Poems*. The alteration
makes the syntax clearer.

Miss Moore begins as often with a specific example in mind,
here a camellia sabina she has seen packed in a jar of French
plum brandy. Typically she states the name of the packer and
specific details of the appearance of the jar, and she remarks upon
the similarity in appearance of the flower and the jam. She
obviously delights in the slightly difficult sound clusters of
the seventh and eighth lines, sounds perhaps intended to parallel
the somewhat prickly imagery in the lines: the camellia is a
"graft-grown briar-black bloom," the liquor is "black-thorn
pigeon's blood." The description of the bottle as having "un-
evenly blown" initials and a green bubble gives details which
in another poem might hint only at a lifelike imperfection but
in this context seem almost to indicate a flaw in ethics. Perhaps too the choice of such words as "graft" and "foil" is intended to imply the idea of deceit: after remarking that the jar
is sealed with foil, the stanza ends with the terse comment
"appropriate custom."

That such a decorative but useless flower was packaged
with what to Miss Moore is misused food is in character. We
are next told that "they"—the French—keep camellias under
glass for study, and practice other "cruel" customs with useful
plants. If Miss Moore is humorous here, she is also at least partly
serious; for she is making artificiality seem, if not quite a sin,
at least a grievous error of perception and understanding. In
elaborating her description of the camellia, she speaks of its

petals as "amanita-white"; the amanita is a poisonous fungus. The third stanza ends with lines detailing the care necessary in some climates to raise camellias, implying that the decorative flower is a fussy one.

The remaining five stanzas present and comment upon the grape and various associations suggested by it. Juxtaposition of these stanzas with those on the camellia is made legitimate, so to speak, by a variety of associations: discussion of both the grape and the flower in the French gardening books that the poem has already made use of; contrast between the "scentless" camellia and the bouquet of grape wines; and the circumstance that certain wines come as red or white, the camellia colors. Miss Moore, no wine-lover, comments that the food grape is the "true ground" for celebration. This remark, seemingly an offhand one, is the theme for the rest of the poem.

Thought of grapes as food brings up the mouse, the "Prince of Tails," who might stroll in a vineyard. Miss Moore's notes to the poem inform us that details of her mouse portrait in the next lines are suggested by photographs. The mouse of one picture is addressed for a few lines in the second person as Miss Moore recites delightedly the jewel-like appearance of grapes placed in his cage, the "Persian" care that has been taken to perfect them and to pluck off the immature. This "jewelry" of sun-gilded grapes is legitimate; that is, it is not meant to deceive, for example, an imagined Tom Thumb who, mounted on a mouse, might wish to look at the grapes in their own reflected light, nor to keep him from dashing around at will in his miniature circus tent. Such grapes are not meant to dazzle and confuse but to serve; the poem seems in this climactic stanza to imply that this makes honest what would otherwise be a dishonest beauty.

The last stanza gives a final dismissal of the spurious. The wine-cellar "accomplishes nothing"; the "gleaning"—the artful care taken in tending and harvesting—is "more than the vintage," of more significance than the end product itself despite showy records of marvelous vintage years. Parentheses enclose two and a half lines intended to jog the reader's memory about the fussy care necessary for the camellia, and the poem ends with a final salute to an Italian grape Miss Moore takes to be a food.

The themes of "The Jerboa" and "Camellia Sabina" appear again in "No Swan So Fine," a short, direct attack, scornful and even sarcastic in tone, on the contrived and false. The opening lines quote a New York *Times* item reporting that no water is so still as that in the dead fountains of Versailles. Similarly, no swan is so "fine" as that on a Louis XV candelabrum tree. That "fine" is sarcastic in intent is evidenced by such details as the description of the swan's glance as "swart blind" and of its body as "chintz china." The very buttons on the candelabrum tree are "cockscomb-tinted"; the hodge-podge of decorations also includes dahlias, sea-urchins, and, ironically, everlastings; the tree's branches are made up of "polished sculptured/flowers"—that is, spurious ones. The poem concludes with the terse sentence "The king is dead." The reader gathers that a king who valued such a contrivance was "dead" before his actual death: to value such artifice is to be spiritually dead. The simplicity of the jerboa demonstrates the restraint characteristic of heroic behavior; the elaborateness of the camellia and the china swan exemplifies the rank grossness of the counterfeit. The hero's vision of "rock crystal" will recognize restraint and reject the false.

The next three poems present exemplifications of the genuine. "The Plumet Basilisk," a long poem in four sections, celebrates the basilisk (*basilicus americanus*) lizard of Central America. To this celebration Miss Moore brings bits of zoological information and oddments of mythological lore; she gives as usual not only presentation of the thing in itself, but also varied samplings of the interpretations man has given it. It is, again, the spirit—the *experience* of the thing—that matters, and it is a compound of the literal and the imagined. She uses neither obvious symbolism, nor much in the way of overt statement; but she provides hints and intimations enough to indicate that the creature stands for the America which the exploitative first settlers failed to find and we of later times have not as yet recognized.

The poem opens with a section of three stanzas under the subtitle "In Costa Rica," a label conveying a certain irony in that the scene is indeed a "rich coast," though not for the reasons the conquering Spaniards assumed. The first stanza employs one of Miss Moore's favorite devices: the seemingly casual beginning that leads with a surprising rightness to the subject. Here the movement is from the "green" of blazing driftwood to the colorings of the fire opal and then to the "living firework" of the basilisk. That this lizard is "amphibious" is significant; as a creature of both land and water, he can represent the total of natural resources. The name "basilisk" comes from the Greek for "king of animals," a point referred to in the second stanza where the lizard meets his own king-like reflection when he jumps into a stream. His launching is described in Keatsian imagery as a process in which he first "faints upon the air"; the implication perhaps is that he leaps less from an act of will than from a kind of natural inclination to merge with his own image. The closing lines of the section that celebrate the lizard's all-round capabilities mix details from the story of El Dorado and from Chinese mythology to indicate a universality of application for the qualities he is meant to represent.

The second section, "The Malay Dragon," and the third, "The Tuatera," continue this universalization and introduce legendry that will be important in the long final section. As we in America have our basilisk, so "they," the Asians, have their Malay dragon; one stanza compares and contrasts the habits of the two. The next stanza (spacing between stanzas one and two is omitted, apparently by oversight, in the *Collected Poems* printing) describes the Malay dragon as the "true divinity" of his land. He is a "harmless god," who can grasp objects while he is in flight and thus, godlike, is seen "conferring wings" on them. He is the "serpent-dove," serpent because of the fable that a lizard-like monster was hatched from a cock's egg by a serpent; yet dove because, as a god, he is a kind of holy spirit. Miss Moore also has in mind the evolutionary theory that birds are of reptilian ancestry, a point further illustrated by the third section's mention of "bird-reptile social life." By the end of the second section the reader is aware that the Malay dragon represents the spirit of his place and is, if not quite a god, at least reminiscent of one. In all this description there is, of course, an implied parallel to the basilisk, a parallel also intimated by the third section that quickly sets down references to various lizards of the world—the tuatera of New Zealand, chameleons, and others—and to carved dragons in Copenhagen which "symbolize . . . security."

Having thus presented the object, the lizard himself together with interpretations of it, Miss Moore was ready to make use of it. Again employing the section title "In Costa Rica"—this time it functions as the first three words of the opening stanza— she suggests the basilisk's airy, spirit-like qualities by remarking on his abilities when alarmed to run on the water and to puff himself up to what he hopes is frightening size even though he seems to weigh no more than a shadow on a bit of silk. (In

CARNEGIE LIBRARY
LIVINGSTONE COLLEGE
SALISBURY, N. C. 28144

line three of the second stanza of this section, "best" is a misprint for "beset.") Lines remarking on the basilisk's serpentine appearance and on his ability to bridge one vine to another are perhaps intended to suggest that he is timeless, the serpent being in some mythologies a symbol of eternity.

The image of a shadow on silk brings up the notion that his barred tail resembles a painting of piano keys; the next several stanzas add to the interplay of factual and mythological allusions a variety of images drawn from musical sounds and instruments. These function as devices for presenting sounds and feelings of the jungle night which could scarcely be communicated literally. The imagery makes the lines as vivid as those that in "The Hero" told what men "shrink" from. This vividness leads to the thought that night in the jungle is itself for man the basilisk of legend, the fearsome monster; but for the basilisk of nature night is the time of most security.

The rhythm quickens as stanza six remarks that, when startled, a "scared frog"—apparently the basilisk himself—may leap into the water and, swimming with an "excellent awkwardness" (because he is, after all, an inhabitant of the shore), can enact the role of a creature that can be "interchangeably man and fish." (*Collected Poems* inadvertently omits the last line of stanza six: "the curve of whose diving no diver refutes. Upon spider-hands, with.") This interchangeability means the basilisk can move up or down like fingers on a harp—up or down, it would appear, the scale of evolution. Passages detailing this movement use short lines and short stanzas, partly to suggest the darting of a lizard in motion but principally to urge intensity of feeling; for these stanzas give the true climax of the poem, an emotional realization of the creature's significances. On the "tightened wires" of a figurative harp, noises grow and change as they will in the "acoustic shell" of the jungle, yet paradoxically the trees, ranked like harp strings, "veil" an "invisibleness" that "ears must feel." This "invisibleness" is—like the trees themselves when seen at night and like the barred tail of the basilisk—of varied black, opal, and emerald shades; and this harmony of lizard, jungle, and the invisible creates an aura of "noiseless music" about the basilisk, here again called a serpent.

Perhaps the reader is being told that time, and the world, have aspects accessible only to a sensitivity that can feel what man cannot hear or see. Yet the basilisk is not a "romantic" symbol. "No anonymous nightingale sings in a swamp," we are told, and

Miss Moore from this point on dismisses musical imagery and returns to the meter of earlier sections of the poem. Not a nightingale but "this," a Central American lizard and all he represents, is the "jewel that the Spaniards failed to see," the life and spirit of America. In the closing stanzas Miss Moore shows him hiding in a lake filled with the precious sacrificial objects that the Spaniards sought but failed to find. Unlike such objects, the basilisk is "alive," despite his "temporary loss" to us. A representative of a spirit in nature and time, he remains a marvelous possibility in a land where exploitation rather than understanding has governed man's relations with nature. Exact definition, apt allusion, and vivid feeling have made the plumet basilisk not a "symbol" but a living embodiment of the spirit of the place.

Another example of the genuine as found in subtropic America is provided in "The Frigate Pelican," a salute to the Caribbean bird of that name as one who can perceive and act without heeding man's commonplace values and his false romanticizing of nature. As printed in *Collected Poems,* the work has five and a half stanzas—just under half of the twelve given in *Selected Poems.* The cutting has considerably improved the poem, for the matter which was dropped elaborated upon the action without adding to it. It is a tribute to Miss Moore's artistic conscience that she could bring herself to eliminate what is, in the context, so fine a line as the opening one of the original twelfth stanza; its polysyllabic words made up of alternately harsh and sibilant sounds perfectly suggested the content: "The reticent lugubrious ragged immense minuet. . . ."

The opening stanza of the *Collected Poems* version describes the bird as "uniting levity with strength"; his levity, it will become apparent, is in his naturalness, his understanding and acceptance of his circumstances. The earlier version contrasted him with a carnival-clad human figure; omitting this contrast enables the poem to deal more directly with the bird. The poem's mixture of fairy tale and fact gives it a suitable levity without destroying its strength of assertion.

Recounting various names applied to the bird, Miss Moore speculates at one point that perhaps "swift" is the proper word for him. The reference is to his speed and to the vagaries of popular ornithology, but it may also imply a comparison of him to the lizard, one of Miss Moore's favorite animals ("swift" is the popular term for one variety of lizard). After presenting his gracefulness, and the almost ceremonious ease of the whole frigate pelican flock in its hovering flight, the harmony with nature in which the flock allows the wind to reverse its direction, Miss Moore herself reverses direction in the third stanza a bit, to remark that these birds are not like the swan that is sometimes, in fairy tales, a servant to man. This comment in turn brings on a statement of typical commonplace "mottoes" of that "less limber animal," man—"Make hay; keep/the shop; I have one sheep." The juxtaposition without transition is typical of Miss Moore's style; it is so handled that it leads not to mere intricacy but to suddenness of revelation. This bird, the frigate pelican, would "not know Gretel from Hansel": he is no slave to the perceptions of deluded man. Like Handel, he "hides" in his "art."

Having remarked upon his "strength," and upon his independence from human ideas and his clever "vigilance," Miss Moore now turns to his "levity." She first quotes the Italian motto that one should be gay civilly and then inquires why this should be advised; her reply is a Hindu saying implying that whether one is blessed or cursed depends not on what others think of him but on whether what he does is good or evil. The bird, that is, is not required to be "civil" in the sense of accepting the judgments of others, for he knows that what counts is what he does. He earns his gaiety by right action. The poem closes with lines presenting an extension of this idea. Men romanticize the moon, for example, whereas this "most romantic" bird sleeps in a swamp hidden from moonlight. But he not only avoids what the poem implies is the merely conventional; he also shows an ability that is to be envied: when crushing danger is near, he wakes from his sleep and escapes it. Thus the frigate pelican stands for what in the context of this poem is to be taken as a true romanticism, an independence of mind and an understanding of nature that are superior to the acceptances and sentimentalizations deluding man.

Though independence from man's notions is admirable, service to him in his workaday world may be honorable. "The Buffalo" opens with speculations on possible symbolisms of the black tones of a bison the poet has seen pictured (three lines omitted from the second stanza in *Collected Poems* made the point that the subject is a print). In the next stanzas Miss Moore reflects upon the evolution from the extinct aurochs to the present-day cow, a development which is something of a descent in biology and, we gather, in value. However, she continues, if we are to consider "human notions," perhaps the "best" creature of the *Bos* genus is the Indian buffalo, a hard-working but independent and spirited animal who is neither customarily bespangled with jewelry like a temple elephant, placidly subservient like a Vermont ox, nor freakish like a painter's imagined animal; he is mettlesome, "free," cheerful, yet capable of fighting off a tiger. His qualities, indeed, are such that he need not feel inferior to "any/of ox ancestry" whether these be the twins of mythology, the aurochs, or the prairie bison. He combines, that is, the virtues of his wild ancestors and of his domesticated contemporaries with those of the oxen of myth. Thus uniting the mundane and the imagined, he is of high value.

"The Buffalo" originally appeared in a magazine together with another poem suggested by a picture, "Nine Nectarines" (*A Marianne Moore Reader* restores the full original title, "Nine Nectarines and Other Porcelain"). In "Nine Nectarines" we see that the objectivist poet, interested in presenting realities, may find the imagined superior to the realistic. The poem contrasts a garden book's poor reproduction of a decorated Chinese plate with a good enameled porcelain picture of a unicorn. The plate is adorned with a painting of nectarines on a twig. The opening stanzas establish the similarity of the nectarines to the peach which in China symbolized and, indeed, was believed literally to afford, long life. But these nectarines, carelessly depicted by the "unenquiring brush" of the commercial publisher in whose "bookbinding" Miss Moore saw the picture, are on a "much-mended" plate—not one blessed with long life—and are reproduced as so unnaturally flawless that one seeing them might doubt that the nectarine was ever a "wild spontaneous" fruit. Miss Moore deftly and somewhat wryly suggests that the garden-book writer supports such doubts by mentioning that he prudently "would not say" whether or not the nectarine was ever domesticated. The demonstration of the inaccuracies possible under the aegis of realism is reinforced by describing the animal also painted on the plate, an animal apparently supposed to represent a real-life creature but one so poorly drawn that it is impossible to tell whether the artist had in mind a moose, horse, or ass.

At this point in the middle of the fourth stanza, the *Collected Poems* printing drops three and a half stanzas from the *Selected Poems* version. The omitted passages elaborated finely upon the plate's decorations and drew an extra contrast between the rather heavy realism of hunting and domestic scenes in European dinnerware and the perfection of Chinese decorators' control of imagined subjects. The material did not advance the movement of the poem, though we may regret losing such a fine passage as the lines descriptive of a bat in moonlight whose eyes "are separate from the face—mere/delicately drawn gray discs, out from/itself in space."

The conclusion in the cut version of the poem, which comes almost abruptly, remarks that the artistry of the enameled kylin demonstrates that the Chinese race is one which "'understands/ the spirit of the wilderness.'" Miss Moore's notes do not give a source for the quotation; we may surmise that this is an instance of her occasional use of quotation marks to hold an observation up for examination and celebration. The ending lines assert that only a "Chinese" imagination, one open to the spirit as well as to the merely literal, could have produced such a masterpiece. Evidence that Miss Moore herself seeks to be faithful to the spirit of the object is the fact that the kylin described in this stanza scarcely conforms in detail to the creature described in her notes to the poem. The nectarine and the kylin had special appeal to Miss Moore as subject matter, for the fruit in its kinship to the peach, and the mythical animal in its embodiment of male and female, both could represent unity. And she sometimes, as in "The Buffalo," seeks subjects that can be made to symbolize unity of matter and spirit. That both nectarine and kylin symbolize long life also made comparison of them possible. Since the examples of these subjects she happened on were not of equal artistic merit, she had opportunity for the pointed contrast that is the basis of this poem.

A proper concept of reality will shape the proper behavior that is the topic of the next three poems. "The Fish" celebrates courageous independence; "In this Age of Hard Trying, Nonchalance Is Good and" recommends intelligent restraint; and "To Statecraft Embalmed" argues that life must be served even if doing so violates decorum. "The Fish," one of Miss Moore's earliest good poems and therefore one of her most celebrated, follows one of her typical patterns of organization. It begins with notation of exact details that surround the object; after a sufficient accumulation of these, it moves to a statement of what they indicate about its nature; finally it gives the ethical significance of its qualities. Though this pattern is simpler than the structures of some of her later work, it is not in broad outline essentially different.

In "The Fish" the chief object is a cliff at the ocean shore. The poem, however, begins not with a description of the cliff itself but with a mention of the fish that move about it. That they "wade," rather than swim easily, perhaps indicates that the very water at the base of the defiant cliff takes from it an aura of resistance. The world in which the fish move is dark; there is a suitable parallel between their presence in the steely water and the existence of a spirit within the cliff itself. The "ash-heaps" of mussel-shells, crow-blue in color, include one shell that opens and shuts itself like an "injured fan," a comparison that gives a vividly accurate picture of such a shell's movements and also suggests the peril and hardship of this stern world. There is no refuge of any sort; the very barnacles "cannot hide," for reflected rays from the sun penetrate the crevices in the rock-torn waters and in the cliff itself, almost as though someone were deliberately aiming a spotlight into the cruel turquoise sea. The water has like a chisel "driven" (not eroded or worn) a chasm into the iron of the cliff itself; there ocean creatures are tumbled one over the other. The colors, the textures, the action of sun and water all suggest mortal danger, implacable if impersonal hardness.

In this appropriate setting the cliff looms scarred by "All/external/marks of abuse . . ." from wave and weather. It bears the marks of human assault from the land too, for its face shows "dynamite grooves" and "hatchet strokes." The "chasm-side"—the face the cliff presents to the water, or perhaps the face of the rent that the waves have driven into the rock—is "dead." Yet, abused though it is, the cliff paradoxically can "live on," can feed its spirit on the harshness that ages it. The assaulting sea, not the resistant cliff, wearies under the strain of the perpetual battle.

The cliff seems to represent for Miss Moore an ideal. Battered by that sea which—as in "A Grave" and "The Steeple-Jack"—symbolizes the peril of existence, the cliff demonstrates the capacity of the courageous in spirit to triumph. Like William Faulkner's mankind, it does not merely survive but will prevail. The *Collected Poems* version of the poem uses a five-line stanza that gives an effect of relatively greater thoughtfulness than the faster-paced six-line stanza of earlier printings.

Though Miss Moore greatly admires the bold endurance that may be wounded but is never worn away, she sees that another kind of value may be necessary in human circumstances. How an artist might proceed is the subject of "In This Age of Hard Trying, Nonchalance Is Good and." This work is one of the few poems in which Miss Moore does not have in mind a well-defined "object"—animal, work of art, scene—to provide her with analogies, allusions, or other sources for the leap of interpretation that brings her to her poem. In this poem the dependence is on an implied story. The situation apparently arises from her speculation upon the quotation from Dostoevski that opens the poem, " 'really, it is not the/business of the gods to bake clay pots' " (she has added the conversational "really" to the quotation). "They," the gods, would not bake pots on one occasion, she tells us; some of them enwrapped themselves in their own egos as though thinking contemptuously that communion with others, "excessive popularity," would be a mere "pot," a worthless goal. The result was that an ability that might have "split the firmament" had no effect. Discarding itself, this power fell on "some poor fool" and gave him a talent for storytelling. His tales were not realistic but, being inspired, were far better than the dull "certitude" of routine talkers.

Perhaps he was something of a reformer in ethics; proceeding by indirection, possibly by such semi-fables as Miss Moore herself is fond of, he was more effective in his "by-play" than were the direct sermonizings of the uninspired. His restraint, therefore, is the best means to the "self-protectiveness" that is a true "weapon" because, we gather, it enables accomplishment that the self-centered behavior of the gods in this story could not achieve. They cut themselves off from others, but desirable self-restraint would result in freedom of perception and truth of expression, not in isolation. The best garb or pose for the self-protective is that of the wanderer who has no alliances that might unnerve him for the campaign he must wage. The long title of the poem, making up the first half of a sentence that is completed in the first two lines of the poem, taken together with the ending, suggests the recommendation that in this age of competitive and obvious effort, an artful casualness is the best manner for the poet.

Yet "nonchalance" in attitude is not to mean evasion of responsibilities, a point demonstrated by "To Statecraft Embalmed," which scolds whoever would recommend discretion as better policy than justice. The poem is an address to the sacred ibis of ancient Egypt. The ibis was often identified with Thoth, the moon-god who in some aspects was regarded as the agent of creation-by-words, the founder of the arts and sciences, and hence the source of wisdom and magic. Mummified remains of the ibis were often therefore placed in the tombs of Egyptian rulers along with secret inscriptions intended to guide and magically protect the dead.

The title, we may note, uses "statecraft," not "statesmanship." The bird-god addressed is apparently mummified, for, under "hard" plumage, he is guarding a secret in a sarcophagus. He is told that there is "nothing to be said for" him, and he is sarcastically advised to conceal his secret. The fourth line consists of only the single-letter word "O," and each fourth line thereafter is a monosyllable rhyming with it: the effect is that of a mocking litany, ironically aping the reverent words addressed to such a bird in ancient Egypt. The bird is a "necromancer," one gifted with the power to talk with the dead and, in the poem, with the power to speak from the tomb. As the god of wisdom, he is asked whether the idea of Justice, perhaps as inscribed or symbolized in the tomb, should be allowed to come to life. Leaving the tomb to respond, the bird-god says no; and he magically winds about "us," his questioners, a "snow" of silence which he deepens with "moribund" talk. What he recommends, it appears, is the "discretion" that statesmen often value above right action.

The poem now editorializes, declaring that such crafty behavior is not in our day "statesmanlike." The bird-god protests that giving embodiment to an ancient "grace" is more important than justice, but the poem replies that life, despite its flaws, is better than decorum: justice is a live quality; decorum may be a dead one. The last nine lines angrily predict that one so out of touch with necessities will fail to see the unreality of his actions; his "suicidal" dreams, perhaps of power and national glory, will drive him to attack his friends and fatally to embrace his foes. This is one of Miss Moore's few poems on political ethics. Even in it, of course, the political element is only a vehicle for conveying the point that in any circumstances justice is to be valued more than discretion; life, more than social propriety.

It is a truism that all poems are "about" poetry. At least the next ten pieces in *Collected Poems* are more or less direct treatments of poetry itself and of the poet and his critics. In "Poetry" Miss Moore states something of her own artistic creed; in "Pedantic Literalist," "Critics and Connoisseurs," and "The Monkeys," she comments upon criticism; in "Melanchthon," "In the Days of Prismatic Colour," "Peter," "Picking and Choosing," "England," and "When I Buy Pictures," she presents particular aspects of her esthetics.

As a statement of objectivism—of the importance of presenting the object for itself and thus paradoxically achieving a heightening that impositions by the writer could not attain—"Poetry" can be compared with Wallace Stevens' poem "Not Ideas About the Thing/But the Thing Itself" and with the proem to William Carlos Williams' *Paterson*. "Poetry" contains Miss Moore's most direct assertion that precise, accurate presentation of the subject will arouse the most—indeed, the only—valid comprehension of it. The beginning assertion that "I, too, dislike it" is sometimes quoted as evidence that Miss Moore is a good sophisticate who does not take her art seriously, that under the skin she is essentially a pleasant, middle-class "intellectual" without unmodish convictions. But to so read her is to read quite wrongly. Though the remark is on the face of it ironic, it is more than a simple comment of obvious indirection. She is declaring her disgust with the common view of poetry as a way of prettifying standard opinions, usually those of intellectual liberalism. The critics who read her as having contempt for all poetry are thus hoisted on their own petard: the kind of poetry she dislikes is, or includes, that which they commonly prefer. What she likes is "the genuine"; the rest of "Poetry" is an effort at explanation of this quality.

She first declares, in lines reminiscent of T. S. Eliot's "The Hollow Men," that vivid presentation of the specific details of a subject is important not because it may lead to "high-sounding interpretation" but because it is "useful": because it can lead to the "genuine." But if these details are only "derivative," removed from the actuality of the experience, none of us will admire them. The "us" is delightfully and pointedly represented as creatures engaged in a variety of activities; the passage deftly scores the "immovable critic" as a horse to whom the work of art is a flea. No one, the poem is saying, is likely to be diverted from his usual concerns by anything other than the accurately presented. All the "us" are possible subjects; even the business and schoolroom documents sometimes excluded from the canon of literary material may be used for poetry.

Yet, as these inclusions would indicate, the mere thing in itself is not a poem: "half poets" who celebrate the humdrum detail for its own sake do not thereby make poetry. What is important is that the poet be true ultimately, not to fact but to his imagination; poets must be "literalists of the imagination," above the insolence of expecting presentation of the trivial to be poetry. The poet must give " 'imaginary gardens with real toads in them' "—a populace of real objects that, taken together, will produce an imagined experience. Perhaps no one at present has achieved such art; meanwhile, one may qualify as being "interested in poetry" if he demands fulfillment of the objectivist paradox that "rawness," the accurate presentation of the thing itself, must be the basis for, the material of, a "genuine" garden which is more than the sum of its physical components.

This theory is, of course, ultimately a neoromantic one; for it requires something more than realism of observation. It does insist, however, that one start from the accurately realized object. In Miss Moore's creed, poetry must climb to heights beyond realism, but it must begin its ascent on a stairway of fact. The enameled kylin of "Nine Nectarines" was a better object of art than the painted fruit, though delineated with perhaps equal inaccuracy, because his creator perceived the spirit within him.

In rhetorical form "Poetry" follows one of Miss Moore's common patterns; moving from an artfully casual beginning to a climax of feeling in the next-to-last stanza, it then ends almost off-handedly with a final, fairly direct comment upon what has been presented. As a work of art, it is its own exemplification. Though it deals more directly with an abstract subject than most of her work, it is grounded on a sufficient quota of such specificities as "hair that can rise," a bat upside down, a "wild horse taking a roll." Because it is provided with these concrete details, it is much more successful than "In This Age of Hard Trying, Nonchalance. . . ," in which the subject is equally abstract but the incident the poem is based upon is not clearly delineated.

Each of the remaining nine poems in this group works through a particular object or set of circumstances. The injunction in "Poetry" that one must be a "literalist of the imagination" does not of course mean approval of the "Pedantic Literalist" who is disparaged in the poem of this title. The chief error of the mundanely minded is illustrated as deceptiveness: his failure to perform what he seems to promise. Such a literalist is termed in the opening line a "Prince Rupert's drop" (a blob of glass so treated that it appears attractive but flies apart when handled) and a "paper muslin ghost," a spurious spirit that would crumple if embraced. A further comparison is to a heart which, failing to give warning of its weakness, caused its owner's death. (In stanza three, *Collected Poems* misprints "pinful" for "painful.") The result of long practice at deception—perhaps of trying vainly and unimaginatively to make poetry out of the merely literal— is that the spontaneity with which even the "literalist" is born turns into wood.

The "hardihood" that resists spontaneities is the topic of "Critics and Connoisseurs," a poem opening with the somewhat resounding remark that there is "a great amount of poetry in un- conscious/fastidiousness." Certain "products" of conscious fastidiousness are "well enough in their way," the poem con- tinues, but such spontaneous attempts at careful procedure as a child's efforts to right a toy and to feed a puppy are better acts of art because they are unforced. Another example of over- done fastidiousness is a swan remembered as reluctant to give up its "disbelief," its false dignity, in order to eat food thrown to it. In the third stanza the poem turns to "you," the critics and connoisseurs who, like the swan, have "ambition without understanding." An illustration of this fault is furnished by the behavior of an ant that foolishly continued attempts to find a use for burdens that could contribute nothing to ant goals. The poem ends with an inquiry: of what use are such ambitions as those of the swan and the ant, ambitions to maintain an impenetrable reserve or to demonstrate that one has struggled for a useless trophy? Remembering the comment in "Poetry" that objects are good if in some sense useful, we may deduce that critics, like the swan, and connoisseurs, like the ant, are guilty of adopting attitudes and of choosing goals that could be valuable if intended to serve some useful purpose but are often clung to without understanding. The poem is recommending more atten- tion to the spirit, less to the letter.

"The Monkeys" makes it clear that, though the artist is to find a "spirit" in the object, his enterprise is not to be an ex- pedition into the "arcanic." The poem, which begins with com- ments upon sights observed during a long-past trip to a menagerie, remarks on the difficulty of recalling in detail the reasons for the impression of "magnificence" that remains. But one creature will not be forgotten, a large, kingly cat who perhaps represents those described at the end of "Poetry" as "interested in poetry." He, it seems, gave the indignant speech of the last two stanzas of "The Monkeys," a protest against critics' imposition of "inarticulate frenzy" and their insistence on almost "malignant" depths in poetry. Miss Moore, an impressionist in her own criticism, is again arguing for the spontaneous rather than the codified and pseudo-profound that she apparently believes typical of the "immovable" critic of "Poetry," the "consciously fastidious" interpreter of "Critics and Connoisseurs."

The ease with which she has a cat deliver a comment, almost a diatribe, on literary criticism demonstrates the art in the seemingly casual beginning and ending which give a rightness to the choice of a feline spokesman. Having an animal convey the message provides a neat irony; the poem's original title, "My Apish Cousins," made somewhat more obvious the ironic comparison of human and animal.

The unimaginative literalist is again a target in "Melanchthon" (discussed in Chapter I of this book), with its closing question, amounting to an assertion, that the depth of a life and of a poet's work will not be perceived by one who fails to sense the "unreason" or mystery that Miss Moore believes to lie behind all experience.

Yet though the poet is not to be "consciously fastidious" and is to see an "unreason," he is nevertheless to be clear. "In the Days of Prismatic Colour" declares that early in creation color was "fine" or exact, not because of art but because of its closeness to its origins. Even "obliqueness," indirection, was apparent and understandable, not hidden. But now the oblique is no longer accessible, and color no longer holds its purity; original simplicity has been replaced by "complexity." Though there is nothing wrong with complexity when it reflects actual perception, it is wrong when indulged in to the point that it obscures. And it is especially wrong when made an end in itself, when a poet values the vehemence instead of the worth of what he is saying, and insists that all truth must be dark. Such insistence, being "principally throat," is a "sophistication" that is the direct opposite to truth.

Sophisticates, it appears, view the truth as something like a monster of Greek myth, crawling, gurgling, and darksome. "To what purpose!", she exclaims, are the perverse misunderstandings that see truth as complex and even as monstrous. Truth is "no Apollo/Belvedere, no formal thing": it is, we gather, spontaneous and unconscious. Though complexity may appear in it, not this but courage and endurance are its chief characteristics. The "wave" of critical fashion, of philosophical challenge, may roll over it; but, like the cliff in "The Fish," it will survive.

The virtue of being "natural," of doing without pretense or alibi what one is designed to do, is celebrated with appropriate playfulness in "Peter," a presentation of a friend's cat and a demonstration of Miss Moore's ability to exemplify in a poem the virtues she is meditating upon in the process of writing it. The observations of Peter she presents are those identified with what might be called his cat-ness: complete relaxation, narrowed eyes, obvious nightmares, and lack of concern with judgments that would condemn him for possessing the claws and tail he was born with. In defending him, Miss Moore implies a contrast with the sophisticated human beings in whose world Peter lives. Remaining unabashed by the "published fact"—his obvious animality—and willing "to purloin, to pursue" as instinct bids him, Peter the cat is a living example of natural behavior. Each moralistic observation arises with artful casualness from a particular set of observations. The tone of the whole is one of gentle reasonableness, maintained by the underlying incongruity of a poetic defense of a cat.

That naturalness is essential for the literary critic, who should see literature as "a phase of life," is the assertion of "Picking and Choosing." The advice is, as in "In the Days of Prismatic Colour," that we should not approach literature with fearful reverence. And, as in the passage in "Poetry" dismissing "half poets," we must not come to it as though it were merely commonplace. In his statement the critic must use the "true" word, avoiding the murky and the faked. As examples of the kind of "fact" that critics should give, Miss Moore presents capsule comments on Shaw and Henry James that mention flaws in their work but also point to virtues. (The comment on James has changed markedly. *Poems* said flatly that James "is not profound"; later versions say that James is all that he is said to be "if feeling is profound.")

Miss Moore concludes the passage with lines observing that Hardy, for example, should be seen not primarily under the stereotype of novelist and poet but as a man conforming to a dictum of T. S. Eliot that one should interpret life through "the medium of the emotions." "The Monkeys" showed Miss Moore's own preference for criticism that has an emotional basis and her scorn for systematic, intellectual methods. She does in "Picking and Choosing" concede that, if the critic must have an opinion, he may be permitted to "know what he likes." The next lines admit Gordon Craig and Kenneth Burke to the rank of good critic, both apparently having impressed Miss Moore as knowing what they like.

Thought of Burke brings up the phrase *summa diligentia,* which Miss Moore translates (in the essay "Humility, Concentration, and Gusto") as "with all speed." These words remind the poet of the schoolboy mistranslation of the Latin as meaning "on top of the diligence," an example of one kind of bad literary criticism. In a tone of reasonableness, the poem then comments that "We are not daft about the meaning" but that the "familiarity" critics exhibit with "wrong meanings" is puzzling. The next several lines address those who exhibit such familiarity, adjuring them that, for example, the simple candle should not be seen as an electrified mechanism.

The last six lines ostensibly are addressed to a dog yapping to the world at large his daydream that he has caught a badger. He is told that he should remember that, even if he had really accomplished the feat, he would scarcely need to make such a clamor about it. The moral is that the critic should give hints, a few spontaneous reactions, not mystification and not boasts of imagined retrievals. The poet is recommending the process named in her title: the "picking and choosing" that she considers to be primarily a task for the emotions, not for powers of abstraction and analysis. We may note that Miss Moore can be reasonably impersonal in her opinions of critics, for her work has been praised since the 1920's by Yvor Winters, R. P. Blackmur, Burke, Eliot, Stevens, and Williams—a range including "new critics," impressionists, and eclectics.

A certain naturalness—lack of apparent artifice—is the quality Miss Moore defends in America, the country that the poem somewhat paradoxically entitled "England" is principally about. Its opening stanzas cite various examples of neatness of finish or of civilized proficiency in Europe and Asia; without transition, the third stanza begins to detail characteristics observed in America, a list not of abstract qualities but of such specifics as the smoking of cigars on the street. The tone of the passage has a playfulness indicative of Miss Moore's affection for the homey detail she is listing. The poem turns serious, however, as allusion to different ways of pronouncing English brings up the assertion that such a matter should not give rise to "continents of misapprehension." The consequent reflection follows that not every mushroom which appears to be poisonous is really unsafe, a metaphor implying that not every American trait is to be condemned without reflection. A listing, so rapidly paced as to seem to tumble out, of great qualities in European and Asian civilization ends with a sarcastic remark that Izaak Walton's concentration on fish is one "flower" of boasted European "superiority." That a person has not perhaps met greatness in America is not proof that it does not exist: it has never been "confined to one locality." The surface of homely fact in America may be deceiving to the Europophile who identifies greatness with conscious fastidiousness, so to speak. The poem's success is due partly to its vivid particularization of national qualities. The novel use of colons in the second and third stanzas, perhaps intended to imply that one detail is strengthened by the next, is also found in the poem "The Labours of Hercules."

To fail to see possibilities in America is to err in perception—to trust in stereotypes instead of in spontaneity of observation. More serious is failure to see what in Miss Moore's opinion are the spiritual forces that lie within all the world of appearances. She made the point in "Poetry," "Pedantic Literalist," and "Melanchthon," and she asserts it overtly in "When I Buy Pictures." This poem lists subjects for painting that would give the poet, surely Miss Moore herself, "pleasure in my average moments." The examples are pictures that would be notable for "intensity of mood" or for charm of content. The passage leads to a dismissal of "Too stern an intellectual emphasis." Further qualifications are that the pleasing must not be an attempt "to disarm," to argue or deceive; and it must not be one of those paintings commonly accepted as masterpieces only because others have not had equal publicity. Whatever the desirable picture may deal with, it must convey emotional insight: it must "acknowledge the spiritual forces which have made it." The somewhat longer, earlier version of this piece given in *Poems* was more obviously insistent on the necessity that a picture arouse an individualistic response in each observer and be the product of a particular artist; apparently Miss Moore felt this early version to be too editorial.

Thus the objectivist poet is qualified as one of the "literalists of the imagination," for he will maintain a spontaneity of reaction and impression; he will reject stereotypes and ponderous systems in order to be open to understanding that can come to him only by faiths and intimations. He is not to show sensory reality because that reality has value in itself, but because, in showing it accurately, he will discover the "spiritual" that informs it. The spirit, that is, is not a mystery; it is as much a part of reality as the material.

Belief in the existence of a spiritual world does not mean that Miss Moore is content with received optimisms. The fact that courage is her principal value, that she thinks the advisable existence to be an armored one, indicates that her world is one wherein danger always threatens. In "The Steeple-Jack" and in "The Fish" the sea was a challenge and threat, a symbol of forces to be resisted with bravery and independence. The ever-present perils of existence are the subject of her poem on the sea, significantly entitled "A Grave." In it the sea is beautiful, tempting, and challenging. But it concedes nothing; it is totally inhuman; and, more than impersonal, it is malign. The poem opens as an address to a man who is apparently blocking others' view in order to look at the ocean himself; his rudeness is an example of the greed that governs men's attitudes. The poem warns him he can expect nothing from the sea but "a well excavated grave." Man's day-to-day environment, represented by a stand of firs, gives no hint of any feelings; but the sea is not a practitioner of such "repression": it returns quickly any "rapacious" looks that are given it. The poem recounts warningly the fate of men who lost their lives in attempting to conquer the sea. On the water's surface cautious men go about their business of netting for fish, not aware that they are "desecrating a grave," acting as though there were no death, yet perhaps betraying a recognition as they row quickly away.

We are not told of any happening, but from the sixteenth line the mood changes. The rest of the poem seems an astringently pitying account of how the ocean, though having perhaps just drowned a man, continues in its age-old, beautiful indifference. The waves move on, the birds and the bell-buoys call, and the ocean deceptively looks as though it were not that sea in which "dropped things" die so quickly that any movement they perform is caused only by its waters. The dangers hinted at in "The Steeple-Jack" have occurred; yet the sea remains as treacherously attractive as ever. The implied moral is not that one should be fearful but that he should be cautious: courage is not fool-hardiness. The perils of existence are perhaps not always appar-ent; but, like spiritual forces, they are real and must be recognized. The reader may be reminded of Williams' poem "The Yachts," which has similarities in idea and execution.

There are, of course, less fatal perils for man. Undue soph-istication is the topic of two poems. In "Those Various Scalpels" Miss Moore presents a woman dressed in high fashion, brilliant but artificial. Having in mind such poems as "No Swan So Fine" and "In the Days of Prismatic Colour," the reader is scarcely surprised to find that aspects of the woman's appearance are compared to stone and ice; indeed, the details are so ludicrously exaggerated that one is reminded of Shakespeare's sonnet spoof-ing "false compare." The woman's appurtenances, designed to rustle "conventional opinion," are "rich instruments" with which to study or experiment with life. But, asks the poet, why do this with instruments more sophisticated than life itself? Life, that is, is relatively simple and frank; understanding of it is open to all who, like the cat in "Peter," are willing to respond naturally.

Sophisticates of various sorts are targets of the series of sarcasms in "The Labours of Hercules." They include such mistaken people as those "of austere taste" who refuse to recognize that creativity demands freedom and as those of "fourteen carat ignorance" who pose as sages. There are, the poem concludes, certain fixed values; for example, "one keeps on knowing" that members of other religions or nationalities are decent people. Uncertainties of punctuation make it difficult to tell whether the tasks of the last seventeen lines are more of the "labours" named in the title, or are ethical missions particularly appropriate to the "creative power" of the immediate-ly preceding passage. Perhaps the uncertainty is deliberate; these chores could appropriately be both Herculean labors and missions for the esthetician of ethics. The poem is essentially a series of citations of errors in attitude or feeling, and each is contrasted scornfully with what Miss Moore feels to be a genuine principle.

The sophisticate sees himself as a member of his society's élite, as one especially aware of fashionable refinements in behavior. Two poems deal particularly with the importance of one's social environment. The first of these, "New York," may be contrasted with Carl Sandburg's famed realistic celebration of his city as "Hog Butcher for the World" in "Chicago." It is not the "plunder" that makes city life important, Miss Moore asserts; it is the "accessibility to experience" that it affords. She selects one aspect of the variety that is New York, its function as the center of the wholesale fur trade. This is useful synechdoche, enabling her in small space to obtain a coherent variety of imagery and metaphor; and it is something more than a merely coy conceit, for furs are obtained at some cost in animal pain and human effort, and function as one of the principal status symbols in our society.

Yet the fur business is not the real city, the one that matters to an aware human being. Indeed, to "go in," to become enthralled by the values of the city as a trade center, is to become "lost"; the glamor and hustle of the fur trade, of commercial life generally, are a "savage's romance," "a dime-novel" exterior." What matters about an environment is not the material powers and advantages it may afford, but the variety of opportunity it offers for some degree of spiritual "experience." Allusions to the fur trade of frontier days and descriptions of the modern city in terms drawn from that trade make for a humor that helps avoid didacticism, and they also suggest an ironic view of New York's boasted status as a cultural center: here, indeed, in the artificial "ingenuity" of commerce is the reason for the city's being.

From consideration of her city she moves to more general reflections in "People's Surroundings." This poem explores the paradox, stated in the opening lines of its final stanza, that men develop behaviors intended to put an artful surface on motivations they may not wish to have exposed; yet, if we see accurately, we discover that appearances are not concealments but rather a guide to the nature of a man. What he does, where he lives, how he builds and furnishes—these are a surface "exterior" to his central self. Yet, as in "Melanchthon," this exterior is intimately linked with the self and is indicative of its nature. The poem opens with four short stanzas presenting types of surroundings people may be found in, from a simple room to a palace, a modern business building, and a wealthy estate. Though the statement of these settings indicates approval of the simple and delight in the colorful, and shows rejection of the sophisticated and the sterile, it functions principally as a demonstration of the variety in human circumstances. The fifth and sixth stanzas present the mind that "moves in a straight line"—the frank, direct mind of Utah or Texas that, despite apparent simplicity, raises perhaps as many questions as it answers. There is also the self-conscious mind whose typical product is the tropical elegance of Bluebeard's Tower with its cruel history, lush gardens and furnishings, memories of fragile ladies, and encouragement of excessive self-analyses. In all these circumstances it is apparent that men's guiding desire has been for a kind of concealment.

The poem ends not with a rhetorical conclusion but with six lines listing roles in human life and another six listing places where these are typically carried out. Despite attempts at concealment, the "exterior and the fundamental structure" are one: captains and cooks are indeed found in camps and dining halls. Miss Moore believes in the existence of a spiritual realm, but she is not a Platonist. As an objectivist she takes the realism of sensory observations to be genuine. She does not deny or denigrate realism; she works through it and, indeed, finds that only in accurate portrayal of it can she successfully hint at or discover whatever may lie behind it.

Appearances may of course be puzzling. "Snakes, Mongooses, Snake-Charmers and the Like" records musings occasioned by a friend's interest in exotic animals from India and particularly in an asp possessed by a snake-charmer. The friend used to be interested in humble animals; but now all his admiration is focused on the asp, at which he gazes as though he were charmed. As the asp stands in its basket, its perfection of shape and its rhythm make even one who dislikes it feel "compelled" to look at it. Speculating about the possible meaning of such a creature, the poem mentions the importance the snake has had in human cultures since antiquity. Conceding that it is as "fine" as its worshipers have held it to be, the poem nevertheless suggests that perhaps the snake was invented to demonstrate or to remind us that when "intelligence in its pure form" has found an endeavor to be "unproductive," it "will come back." Perhaps the intimation is that the snake is a reminder of the Garden of Eden, a sign of guilt that has been left to warn that, if man turns out in the long run to be an "unproductive" development in the universe, intelligence may erase him and start creation over again. The question can't be answered; all that we can be sure of is the snake's perfection of form. There is no point in protesting the friend's fascination or the existence of the snake.

Attempts to correct people or circumstances that we do not understand often spring from pride; the best policy is to allow free expression to a "distaste" that, being natural, is not prideful. Distaste here may be thought of as a natural reaction because of the enmity that Genesis reports the Lord ordained between woman and snake.

Two satires on types of writers also deal with the relationship between appearances and reality. "Bowls," which reports pleasure in the sight of lawn bowling, compares it with the meticulous art of Chinese lacquer carving and says that survival of a game with so much punctilio enjoins us in our day to be "precisionists" rather than hasty "Pompeians" whose panic is as permanent as the lavas of Vesuvius, though our letter-writing would suggest us to be panicked indeed. The intention is obviously sarcastic; it may also be ironic, for we cannot help remembering that in bowling the pattern of pins is suddenly disrupted. The impression of irony is reinforced as we read that the speaker of the poem, having reluctantly decided that as precisionists her contemporaries are worth some attention, reports her resolve to answer the questions she receives in the mail from them. But the questions now solemnly cited (why do you like winter better than summer?) are evidence that the correspondents are indeed hasty priers for the trivial. The speaker will answer quickly, for in so doing she "gives twice." The adverb perhaps implies that she will satisfy the interrogator while his interest is alive; perhaps it also hints that she will give a double response, one containing both a straightforward reply and some of the reproach the questioner often deserves.

"Novices" is an attack on fashionable litterateurs who proclaim themselves to be the "good and alive young men." They do not think it necessary for writers to be familiar with what they are talking about; they engage in excessive and pompous analyses of deliberately abstruse work and hold themselves superior to writers who draw on simple sources. Such novices are, in a word, sophisticates. Heedless of the matters of diction, tone, and substance which should interest them, they indulge in inanity and in vapid praises of writers they do not understand. The poem closes with a passage that sets down the ocean-like virtues of Hebrew, a language Miss Moore cites as one example of the kind of knowledge needful for a writer that novices refuse to acquire. The poem is notable for its imaginative, specific presentation of the faults it is condemning and of the contrasting virtues of the Hebrew that represents any "spontaneous unforced passion" that is genuine.

One of several qualities novices lack is the discipline that not only is an important value in Miss Moore's ethics but also is frequently her subject for a poem. The paradox that liberty may be bred by self-discipline, a restraint in action and expression, is explored in the long poem "Marriage." The tone is somewhat humorous, sympathetic yet at times mockingly ironic; the strategy, unusual for Miss Moore but appropriate in this poem, includes a report of an imagined dialogue between an Adam and Eve who are not so much the characters of the Garden of Eden as representatives of married woman and man. The lines are fairly short, usually six to eight syllables; lines of twelve or more syllables are usually followed by lines of four or five. The tone, the mixture of dialogue and speculation, and the brief line allow variety and much wit and paradox.

After an opening passage of seventeen lines commenting on the seriousness of marriage and pondering what the original Adam and Eve might think of the institution by now, longer passages introduce an Adam and Eve of the present, struggling with the human complexities that, the poem says, psychology cannot explain. Eve is talented, changeable, and is said (in lines reminiscent of Robinson Jeffers, the only such passage in Miss Moore's published work) to be possessed of an almost suicidal beauty. This reflection leads to recollection of her role as "the central flaw" in Eden—as the cause of "that lamentable accident" which exempted Adam from primary blame for man's loss of the Garden, an exemption Miss Moore as a woman of course makes a point of referring to with sarcasm. Like Eve, Adam has a beauty that, the poem tells us, is properly celebrated in certain works of art. Adam has been a prophet and sage; but he has failed to observe the unpredictable qualities of woman, he has taken an undue pride in the reverence some have paid him, and he has let himself be dazzled into marriage, a state that is a "trivial" source for the disruption of the grand role he has enjoyed.

Once married, a couple finds that the counsels of Hymen, the marriage god, will be of no help. For example, his advice that marriage late in life is best is of little aid to those who presumably have wed at the customary age. Man and wife must recognize that friction is to be expected and perhaps even valued, for it is a way of testing experience; they must learn at some pain the difference between independence and bondage, and they must accept inevitable differences in opinion and in desires. There follows a dialogue between Eve and Adam, each presenting favorite accusations against the other. The conversation ends with the poem's comment that each loves himself rather too much and that they are "poor" as long as this is true— poor, we may deduce, in peace and in the strength a better understanding of each other could give them.

The concluding issue is stated in the inquiry as to what can be done for such "savages" who frustrate all but the most visionary of those who would like to help them. It is obviously rare that a marriage joins two whole-souled opposites who instead of feuding can reinforce each other. Indeed, so ideal a marriage is so unlikely that the possibility of it is for a moment mocked in lines comparing it to Columbus' demonstration with the egg. Yet, though improbable, such a "charitive Euroclydon," such an impersonal though passionate love, is still the ideal; it would develop a "disinterestedness" that "the world" hates but may nevertheless be found in those with "simplicity of temper." An example appears in an old-fashioned wedding picture. The photographed couple's sturdy individualism of pose, obvious simplicity, and forthright reliance on principle (indicated by a Bible in the foreground) illustrate that paradox verified, so to speak, in the closing lines by allusion to Daniel Webster: the paradox that we must somehow in marriage, as elsewhere, respect and win both liberty and union. The political allusion serves to give the statement application not only to the marriage partnership but to life generally. We must somehow unite in our lives a proper care for the physical with a due recognition for the spiritual in all experience.

"Marriage" is atypical in dealing with an intangible circumstance that Miss Moore could not effectively represent by means of an object or an animal. Possibly because of her "restraint," her desire to keep herself out of the situation, she set down her details with so little explanation that several passages are elliptical. The poem lacks the intensity of, for example, parts of George Meredith's "Modern Love" series; such intensity, however, might be out of place in what is essentially a witty, ironically pitying commentary. In such later poems on the theme of self-discipline as "What Are Years?" and "Nevertheless," Miss Moore becomes more directly editorial. The subjects in these poems, however, are simpler. "Marriage" is complex at least partly because the relationships it discusses are complex.

Since true self-discipline will allow liberty, it is not to mean mere "neatness of finish." It must embrace diversities, a point illustrated by the study of a wild mountain in "An Octopus." The peak, Big Snow Mountain, seems to be a feature of no actual range but a composite of qualities gleaned from handbooks of mountaineering and from pamphlets on national parks. Though it is "deceptively reserved and flat," and has arms "misleadingly like lace," the mountain is an enormous formation of valleys, forests, glaciers, and snow-dunes; it is home to the porcupine, beaver, bear, and goat; it meets the demands of weatherbeaten roamers, ignorant tourists, and holidaying businessmen. Nearly five pages of *Collected Poems* are given to this description, in which the details as usual are particularized vividly, and such attitudes as irony, sarcasm, and humor appear in appropriate passages: this is very much a Marianne Moore mountain, not a guidebook mountain. Just before the one stanza break, the *Selected Poems* version gave an additional thirty-two lines. Most of these described flowers found on the mountain; apparently when preparing *Collected Poems* Miss Moore felt that her presentation had a magnitude suited to its subject without these lines.

The omitted lines, however, also mentioned the naturalness of a bluejay on the mountain, one element in the description being that he knew no Greek. Contrast between characteristics and activities associated with the mountain and the insistence of the ancient Greeks on what are here represented as light, excessively sophisticated ideas, takes up the next page and a half of the poem. The Greeks, referred to as "grasshoppers," enjoyed "delicate" activity, not invigorating mountain sports; they liked "smoothness," distrusting such "complexities" as those represented by the varied elements of the mountain and seeking to produce a simple definition of even so elusive a quality as happiness. Their artificial "wisdom" was "remote" from the practicality displayed by the wardens of the mountain's game preserve—men whose rules forbidding visitors to drink, gamble, or disobey seem a "sarcasm" on the abstract speculations of the Greeks. It is "self-evident," the poem says, that one must be restrained, obedient, and Spartan in behavior if he would match the strength of the peak.

Like Henry James, the mountain is "damned" and neglected

by the public because of the rigor of its demands. The public thinks that James tried only for "neatness of finish," failing to see the difference between his "restraint" of passion and a mere decorum. Similarly the public abhors or avoids the mountain because it is not easy of access. It is neither a classic polish nor a crowd-pleasing smoothness that distinguishes the mountain, but "relentless accuracy." The poem ends with nineteen lines vividly particularizing this "accuracy": the mountain's quality of being exactly what it was designed to be, of existing without reference to abstractions or interpretations or judgments that human beings might make from or about it. The mountain is an exemplification of that objectivist ideal, the thing which is precisely what its self directs it to be. No mythical Olympus of the gods, it is a realistic, geological mountain in all its mountain-ness.

The need for a discipline that will allow freedom for the self within a spiritual and physical partnership is asserted in "Marriage"; the rigor that preserves wholeness of being is admired in "An Octopus." In "Sea Unicorns and Land Unicorns" Miss Moore combines allusions to actual and mythical creatures with elements of religious symbolism to celebrate the unity of the spiritual and the material that, in such poems as "Melanchthon" and "When I Buy Pictures," she deems to be the essence of reality. The first forty-three lines present and comment upon the "fourfold combination" of land and sea unicorns and of land and sea lions found on medieval maps and tapestries as well as in legendry. The sea unicorn (the narwhale of the Arctic, a tusked whale) and the sea lion are the origin of the fabulous beasts that decorate ancient marine maps, the poem tells us; the two creatures are associated in milieu even though the sea unicorn devours the sea lion. And though the land lion is an enemy of the land unicorn, legendry says that these beasts also seek out the same dwelling areas. These associations despite hostility prove a certain "unanimity," the poem tells us, and lines twenty-three to twenty-seven observe delightedly the strength which opposing personalities gain through unity. The creatures, it would seem, have in some respects the kind of partnerships suggested in "Marriage" as ideal though almost unattainable.

Unicorns and lions also are frequently associated in embroideries, especially those making use of the British royal arms (which picture the unicorn of Scotland facing the lion of

England). Like cartographers' embellishments, these designs
are likely to include the sea unicorn of maritime Britain and
the land unicorn English explorers thought indigenous to the
Americas, as well as the sea lion of Britian's Pacific possessions
and the land lion of heraldry. The passage ends with the land
varieties of unicorn and lion facing each other rampant on the
tapestry, as they do on the British arms. The four creatures
in their varied combinations, the poem comments, make "an
odd fraternity." These combinations, together with the creatures'
world-wide range and the mixture of allusions to the real
and the legendary, suggest that the intention is to represent
oneness amid apparent diversity—an idea linked in Miss Moore's
system with unity of physical and spiritual experience.

The last thirty-nine lines of the poem give a delighted
presentation of the land unicorn's magical abilities. The lines
open with a passage making casual reference to the lion of
St. Jerome, a beast associated in legendry with the resurrection
of Christ; Miss Moore makes use of this legendry in her later
poem "Leonardo da Vinci's." The unicorn can elude all ordinary
huntsmen by such feats as throwing himself head foremost from
cliffs. The poem retells the medieval belief that he could be
captured only by placing a virgin in the forest to lure him out
of hiding. This story was taken to be a parallel to Christian
belief; the unicorn represents Christ drawn to the virgin's womb,
betrayed and slain by man, but risen again. The land unicorn of
Miss Moore's poem thus perhaps represents Christ; the import
would be that only the humble and innocent may expect to
receive Christ. Because the unicorn or Christ has great strengths,
miraculous powers, the ideal union of those seemingly "much
opposed" would be a partnership of this figure with the gentle
virgin. Since the land unicorn represents the broad range of
creatures discussed earlier in the poem, the application is also
more general: only the innocent, those with a true humility,
may hope to comprehend the fundamental oneness of the
spiritual and the material.

That such unity is suggested by harmony with one's milieu is
indicated in "The Monkey Puzzle." This name is one sure to
interest Miss Moore, especially since it is the appellation of a
tree (the "monkey pine" of the Chilean coast). The poem
presents the defiant impenetrability, the resistance to straighten-
ing, that make the tree seem to have deliberately chosen the
loneliness of its environment. No one takes it from its lost woods,

though there is a "quilled" beauty in its "complicated starkness." The real puzzle, however, is neither the tree's twisted form nor its determined resistance and isolation; it is the reason for its existence. No explanation can be given, the poem concludes, because "we prove, we do not explain our birth." Not words but living gives the true exposition of inner nature. Like the cliff in "The Fish" and the mountain in "An Octopus," the tree in its triumph within a harsh environment seems to embody qualities of spirit.

Deliberate variation in style between the first and second stanzas is probably the most noticeable characteristic of "Injudicious Gardening," another poem on the theme of privacy. The notes indicate that the situation parallels or was suggested by an exchange of letters between Robert Browning and Elizabeth Barrett. The reader of this poem should observe also the somewhat stronger statement of the second stanza in the earlier version printed in the original *Selected Poems.* The speaker in the poem remarks in the first stanza that he will continue to like yellow roses despite the fact that a dictionary of flowers says roses of this color symbolize infidelity. This stanza is simple in diction and in phrasing. The second stanza, however, becomes Latinate and intellectual, a change which offends the usually approving critic Randall Jarrell (*Poetry and the Age*). The speaker admits that the sense of privacy of the person he is addressing may "deprecate" the offense that his planting of yellow roses might give to those who take flower lore seriously and may therefore consider his action an "effrontery." We may note that Miss Moore doubtless approves of the idea in the first stanza, and she probably disapproves of the concession to artificiality that the speaker is making in the second. Though she values privacy, it can hardly be an excuse for violation of naturalness. The speaker's gardening may be somewhat playfully termed "injudicious" for flaunting conventional symbolism; but his concessions are injudicious in a more serious way.

The thought of the second stanza is as complex as its language. Complexity in thought does not necessarily require complicated expression, of course; but matching expression to content can be a useful poetic device. Miss Moore frequently changes her diction to suit her content; and, as in this poem, she sometimes indicates approval by simplicity and disapproval by complexity. Examples are the variations in " 'Nothing Will Cure the Sick

Lion but to Eat an Ape,'" and, as Hugh Kenner has noted (in *The Art of Poetry*), those in "The Swan and the Cook" in her *The Fables of La Fontaine.*

Miss Moore used one-syllable lines in "To Statecraft Embalmed" to speed the pace of her satire. She makes frequent use of such lines in "To Military Progress," with the result that the words seem to drip down the page almost like drops of blood. This poem, a satire on the concept named in its title, scorns it as so stupid that it fails to see its own suicidal nature. This nature is indicated by the picture of military progress gloating even as the battlefield crows feed on its torso. These crows search for "the lost/Head": such progress is, indeed, brainless. The reader may speculate that the "military" of the title could be intended to apply to the notion of any material "progress"—to hint that he may lose his essential self if he becomes engrossed in the competitive pursuits necessary to achievement of what most call progress.

The last nine of the *Selected Poems* pieces, as given in the *Collected Poems* printing, provide a series of comments on esthetics and on behavior, topics related in Miss Moore's ethics. Such relationships are cited in the opening lines of "An Egyptian Pulled Glass Bottle in the Shape of a Fish." The bottle combines satisfaction of a practical need, the moral quality of "patience" that was necessary in its maker, and the art needed to complete it. It is thus appropriate for celebration by simile and metaphor. In shape it is like a wave, rising to a crest; in color it provides the "spectrum" seen in the scales of a fish. It is an object of obvious attraction for Miss Moore.

Failure to see the perfection of such an object, unless an explicit statement of it is given, is humorously satirized in "To a Steam Roller." The critic, reader, or poet himself who insists on an "application," a direct statement of moral or other meaning, may be said to "lack half wit" and to see no differences among works of art. If it were possible for anyone to be "impersonal," to be dispassionate in esthetic judgment, it would be such a person. It is not to be expected that this person would be attended by a butterfly, would ever, for example, exhibit a spirit of imaginative independence. Yet if there is such a "complement," such a completion of seemingly dull sensitivity, it is vain to question its "congruence." We may recall the remark at the end of "The Monkey Puzzle" that existence is established not by words but by being.

What the critic should see, we are told in "To a Snail," is that good art results from following inner principle. Being informed by principle, good style is neither ornamental nor accidental. Compression, for example, is a virtue related to modesty. It is, we deduce, a device for achieving the restraint Miss Moore values. Such a device is not an "acquisition," not a mere "incidental quality"; it is as natural to the work of the inspired artist as the horn of the snail is to its bearer. The tenth line, which seems to apply particularly to Miss Moore's own metrics, says that if "feet" are not present there should be "a method of conclusions." If the poet does not follow a traditional metrical pattern, he must develop another means of giving movement to his presentation; he cannot give a merely static picture.

The critic who perceives well may detect error and yet go too far in his attempts at correcting it. The one-sentence anecdote given in the ten lines of " 'Nothing Will Cure the Sick Lion but to Eat an Ape' " suggests this when it tells of a man who once detected a "hollowness" of attitude—perhaps in certain works of art—that beauty itself could not redeem. But he took a "disproportionate satisfaction" in his discovery; since vanity under any circumstances results in a lack of decorum, he expressed himself in a wildly "denunciatory/upheaval." The result was that, though he correctly condemned a mistake, he succeeded not in restoring usefulness but in smothering his audience with his "fresh air." The title, quoted from Carlyle, is therefore ironic: surely there is a less violent way of curing the illness of the lion. The expression in one sentence does not result in breathlessness, for the length of phrasings and the use of multi-syllabled words slow the reader down; at the same time, the grammar produces a desirable tautness in statement.

"To the Peacock of France" shows Molière as a wise artist who perceived the society of his time accurately and did well what was necessary to do. Deducing correctly the pattern his talents would have to follow for him to succeed, he made himself appear an appropriate "golden jay" and took on when necessary even the colors of the clown Scaramouche, a "black-opalescent dye." He was not a libertine, for he only kept pace with the moral expectations of the times; his "first adventure"—probably a reference to his affair with Madeleine Béjart, a woman he was long associated with but did not marry—was his own concern, not a matter for the rest of us to judge him upon.

Allusion to his having in this "adventure" a "repertory" seems to imply that his behavior in it was theatrical. The second stanza asserts that Molière's sensible attitude was also observable in his playwriting. Though as a man of his world he was a "peacock," not an anchorite in a cell, he wrote good plays without "horrifying sacrifice of stringency." He used the theatrical conventions of his time to win favor with the king and, more important, with the public, arousing a "spontaneous" delight by the display of his "broad tail," his showmanship. Frivolity of exterior was a necessary protective device; in adopting it Molière was showing the wisdom of spirit that made him an artist.

A poet who believes in the need for inspiration is likely to hold that fundamental principles of art are much the same regardless of the age one lives in. In "The Past Is the Present" Miss Moore shows her belief that, though style and manner change, there are permanent esthetic virtues. Since she herself occasionally uses "external action" and frequently uses rhyme, we are not surprised to find reference to contemporary belief that these qualities may be "effete" and "outmoded" placed in an "if" clause. Conceding that the taste of the moment may oppose them, she will "revert" to Hebrew poetry (a literature she praised in "Novices" for its oceanic virtues). Quoting a speaker who has remarked that Hebrew poetry is "prose with a sort of heightened consciousness," Miss Moore adds that "ecstasy affords/the occasion" for poetry and that "expediency determines the form." The poet, that is, writes as the result of an inspiration, and he uses whatever form he finds convenient, whether because it has been furnished by a tradition or, as with Miss Moore, has resulted from his own labors. Early versions of the poem had quotation marks around this comment also. Removing them means the remark is not presented as the poet's own words, making it seem more persuasive than it did as a report at second hand. Recent printings also omit an italicized introductory stanza that appeared in *Others*.

The revelation afforded by unconscious inspiration is amusingly illustrated in " 'He Wrote the History Book.' " The title quotes a small boy's remark giving a sudden insight into his father's character, casting a ray of "whimsicality" on his father's "mask of profundity." The remark briefly but cogently contributes to our understanding that his father's character includes a fair measure of self-importance. The boy's reasoning is "synthetic," moving straight to what is to him a reasonable conclusion, and is to us an indication of his father's artificiality.

How whimsicality may mask profundity is a theme of "Sojourn in the Whale," a poem celebrating Ireland as an example of the defiant independence Miss Moore admires in "The Fish" and in "An Octopus." The Irish, she says, often pursue wrong tactics and have long been "swallowed" by the English. They have had to listen to insulting assertions that their country has a weak temperament and that, blind and incompetent, it will eventually be "compelled by experience" to give in to the demands of its conquerors that it accept a status of inferiority because "water seeks its own level." But Ireland, the poem concludes, is not motionless; it will one day overcome the obstacles now facing it and "rise automatically." The title implies that Ireland now is in the situation of Jonah when he was riding about in the whale: it is only temporarily a captive of the English cetacean. And the poem also playfully reminds the reader of more recent traditions of "a Jonah" as a nuisance, if not an outright danger, to those who harbor it. This poem is briefer, less analytical of Irish temperament, and less complex in expression than the later "Spenser's Ireland."

Selected Poems ends appropriately enough with "Silence," an examination of the profundity in decorum. "Superior people," the poem tells us, do not impose on others; they are self-reliant to the point that they can occasionally enjoy solitude, and they have a depth of feeling that causes them to become speechless when someone else's speech has delighted them. This is not "silence," the speaker now decides, but "restraint"; it is not a morose or rude unwillingness to participate, but a decorum that avoids effusions and demands for attention. The last two lines present and comment upon another quotation, "Make my house your inn." This invitation is not "insincere," because "Inns are not residences." That is, the speaker himself exemplifies the kind of restraint he values: when inviting others, he makes it civilly clear that their stay is to be for a reasonable period of time. Restraint to Miss Moore means self-reliance, and it means thoughtfulness. It is not what Freudians call repression, but rather a discipline making possible the only valid expression of one's self. Restraint in expression is a necessary counterpart to the armoring she recommends, for if one is not to be imposed upon by others he most certainly should not himself make impositions. Restraint, "silence," has even a spiritual function: Miss Moore recommends it in her essay "If I Were Sixteen Today" because, she says, if one keeps his tongue still he may hear "promptings from on high."

II *Discarded Poems*

Miss Moore omitted from *Collected Poems* four works printed in the original *Selected Poems*. One of these, "Roses Only," seems quite as good as some others she preserved. It has what is, perhaps, too prose-like a beginning, and it includes one awkward nominative expression ("the without-which-nothing of pre-eminence"). But it has a clear movement from beginning to end; and, as a treatment of the paradox that beauty is sometimes a liability rather than an asset, that thorns may be the best part of the rose, it is suited to her attitudes and themes.

The other omitted pieces are all somewhat less clear than Miss Moore's usual work. "Is Your Town Nineveh?" gives two stanzas addressed to someone who feels "desolate," who perhaps has been quelled in an attempt to assert a freedom. The poet asks him if he feels that New York, his city, is Nineveh and he himself Jonah; the lines apparently are intended to recall to the reader the ruin that overtook the Assyrian capital and the bad luck associated with Jonah (whose reputed tomb was in Nineveh). The poet herself has been "by the aquarium," has been like a Jonah and has longed for freedom: she has known the feelings she recognizes in the one she is addressing. The poem is somewhat flat, and the circumstances of its first stanza are not precisely given.

" 'The Bricks Are Fallen Down . . . ' "—the full title has twenty-one words—is a twelve-line piece apparently meant to celebrate a people who, accepting their inability to eliminate war, ceased to fear it. As it stands in *Selected Poems*, it attempts to make its assertion by means of the negative phrasing that is one of Miss Moore's favorite devices for indirection. The negatives in this poem, however, are mistaken; the people, we are told, "did not say" that they would *not* be intimidated by troubles. The words making up the long title of the poem appeared as a passage in an earlier poem, "Feed Me Also River God," which Miss Moore has also discarded. Somewhat tangled negatives also make for difficulty in "Like a Bulrush," the fourth omitted piece; and the nature of its subject is not clear.

Miss Moore omitted from *Selected Poems* itself, and has never reprinted, a number of other poems she had published in the years before 1935. Of the thirteen poems she printed in the Bryn Mawr literary magazines *Tipyn O'Bob* and *The Lantern* from 1907 to 1909, she has reprinted only "Progress" (in *O to Be a Dragon,* under the title, "I May, I Might, I Must"), and "To a Screen-maker" (in *Poems* as "He Made This Screen"); she parallels the opening lines of one other, "Ennui," in a passage in "The Plumet Basilisk." Miss Moore apparently regards most of these works as juvenilia. The reader will agree that most have lamenesses in expression which make not reprinting them advisable.

These poems demonstrate, however, that some of Miss Moore's characteristic concerns developed early. There are poems on pride ("Tunica Pallio Proprior"); on the need for art to be exact in perception ("Qui s'excuse, s'accuse"); and on the superiority of sensory experience to verbalization ("My Senses Do not Deceive Me"). In "Progress" and "Ennui" some of the terseness of expression she later developed is apparent; and in "My Lantern" she experimented with the one-syllable line. But most of the poems are academic imitations of the post-Victorians. We can hardly believe that Miss Moore thought herself to be writing anything other than exercises when she turned out the drinking song "Under a Patched Sail" and the sailor love song "The Sentimentalist."

Experimentation with forms and subjects is also obvious in Miss Moore's early professional verse. There, as in her Bryn Mawr work, she was occasionally susceptible to a neoromantic excess, to prettified *fin de siècle* rhyming. This flaw is apparent in such work as "That Harp You Play So Well" (1915)—addressed to David the psalmist and filled with phrases like "what boots the art"—and in "Counseil to a Bacheler" (1915), four lines of quasi-Early Modern English. At this period she was not yet always able to achieve a presentation of indirection. Thus "The Wizard in Words" and "George Moore" (both of 1915) fail to convey genuine irony because they rely upon prettiness and polish rather than upon vigorous insight. The irony in "Masks" (1916) is commonplace; a much revised version of this poem, appearing in *Observations* as "A Fool, A Foul Thing, a Distressful Lunatic," is more concrete but it still lacks freshness. The sarcasm of "You Say You Said" (1918) is didactic, and the poem's phrasing is not clear.

The fullest representation of her early work is *Observations* (1924), which reprints most of the verse she had published to that date, including twenty-one of the twenty-four pieces given in *Poems* (1921). *Observations* omits from the works in *Poems* only "To William Butler Yeats on Tagore," "He Made This Screen"—both conventional rhyming pieces—and "Feed Me, Also, River God," which approaches Miss Moore's later stance of careful thoughtfulness but has an uncharacteristically abrupt, almost flippant, ending.

Of the fifty-three poems in *Observations*, forty-three reappear in one or another of Miss Moore's later books. Uncertainties in rhythm, syntax, and attitude doubtless occasioned Miss Moore's decision not to reprint some of the discarded ten. Thus "Radical" is flat and a bit halting in rhythm; "Reinforcements" is prosaic; "Talisman" may have seemed to Miss Moore herself to falter because of the objections Eliot voiced to it in his Introduction to *Selected Poems* (that it is "commonplace" in sentiment and inaccurate in its description of a sea gull). We might wish, on the other hand, that Miss Moore would restore "Dock Rats"; it gives a colorful celebration of sensory delights of place and a comment on the superiority of desires for such experience to motives of "expediency." The poem as it first appeared in Alfred Kreymborg's *Others for 1919* was in a slow-moving five-line stanza; but, as revised to a four-line stanza in *Poems*, it moves with appropriate deftness. Also worth reviving—though some clarification in their syntax is needed—are "To a Prize Bird" (earlier "To Bernard Shaw: a Prize Bird") and "To a Strategist": both have color and point.

CHAPTER *3*

Armor for Use: Middle Period Poems

MANY OF THE THIRTY additional poems Miss Moore printed in *Collected Poems* (1951) have as themes discipline and courage, values always honored in her work but perhaps somewhat more on her mind with the approach and subsequent outbreak of World War II. She re-emphasizes the need for captivity by strong belief, insisting that only the man possessed by faith can act in freedom, can sustain the discipline necessary for heroic behavior. Changes in emphasis and additions to her ethics do appear, however. In her early work she would sometimes reprove, even scold her fellow man; now though she continues to keep her guard up, to operate, as one title puts it, "in distrust of merits," she begins to consider that perhaps she must go out actively for "Victory" if she is to achieve it. She becomes less directly corrective, more understanding of man's moral handicaps and thus of his moral possibilities. She still recommends armoring of the self, but this is to be less the aloof defiance represented by the cliff in "The Fish" and more a steeling from within: the whole armor of the Lord, advised in Ephesians, is worn not to enable withdrawal but to fortify endeavor; courage itself becomes a spiritual quality. Finally, in these works of what we may term a middle period, Miss Moore adds to her exposition of values three abstract or ultimate qualities she had not dealt directly with before—love, beauty, and spiritual grace. These changes reinforce determination to become more affirmative. They demonstrate greater confidence in power of poetic exposition and greater assurance in belief.

It is difficult to know whether changes in style are matters of technique or are responses to differing needs of expression. In this middle period there is relatively little of the Latinate diction that appeared in some of Miss Moore's early work; the juxtapositions are still clever, but commonly less abrupt; and

[85]

words very rarely break in the middle to maintain accuracy in syllable count or to achieve a rhyme. The effect of these alterations is to give the poems an air of ease, to intimate a subdued, graceful humor without undue mockery or irony. Though the style retains its cleverness and its wit, these poems do not defy; their tone is that of a quietly reasonable invitation to take part in a consideration of the subject. But these qualities may also be found in some of her early poems; their dominance in this period does not necessarily represent so much a change in stylistic principles as a shift in strategy.

She does in these poems sometimes give more direct editorial comment. In *Selected Poems* the typical work was tied to one bird, beast, cliff, or other "object"; the poem developed in terms of this, by analogy with it and allusion to it. Even in such fairly complex poems as "Nine Nectarines" and "Melanchthon," the consideration was associated firmly with a particular set of objects. But now she sometimes—as in the title poems "What Are Years?" and "Nevertheless"—breaks away from attachment to a "thing." Passages in both these poems allude to a variety of objects that serve a purpose at the moment; both poems ground their cautionary generalizations firmly in sensory realities. But neither allows one object or set of objects to govern its expression. Even in such a less urgent poem as "Rigorists," the "thing," the reindeer, functions as a source for allusions but does not govern the poem. Miss Moore's frequent comments keep us from letting presentation of the creature dominate our minds. The very titles suggest the change. *Observations* indicated poetry making a comment based upon a perceived thing; but *What Are Years* raises an abstract question, and *Nevertheless* seems to suggest continuation of a meditation.

I *Years: An Opportunity*

The first volume of this period was *The Pangolin and Other Verse* (1936); but, since all four of its poems reappeared in *What Are Years* (1941), they may conveniently be considered part of it. All of the fifteen poems in *What Are Years* had previously been published in magazines or books. The third volume of this period was *Nevertheless* (1944). In *Collected Poems* Miss Moore also printed nine poems of these years that had not appeared in books.

That life is a moral experience best confronted with courage is the suggestion of the opening lines in the title poem "What Are Years?" Being only human, we are "naked," we have an "innocence" that leaves us open to error. If our condition is a plight, we nevertheless endure it because we have courage, the heroism to survive and to be "gay" though in "resolute doubt" and even in defeat. Such courage, a quality more spiritual than physical, arises from the will. It is a choice one makes; it is the vision of the man who "accedes to mortality," not as a coward, but as one who recognizes that his human condition is an entrapment from which there is no escape for him as a living being. Yet he struggles because he knows too that he possesses a spirit which demands heroic behavior of him. "Mortality" lies about us; yet, like the waves of the sea, we survive because we continue to struggle.

The human being who feels strongly thus "behaves" heroically. Like the bird who sings though caged, he will get along without "satisfaction"—the relatively trivial delights of an impossible freedom—because he can live in "joy" of spirit. To give in, to become cowed, would be to accept mere "mortality"; to behave heroically is to recognize eternity, is to respond to the more than mortal spirit within us. "Years," then, are a chance to build mettle, to prove in action the inspirations of spirit.

The theme of struggle as essential, of the trapped paradoxically being free, is most fully treated in "What Are Years?" but is common in Miss Moore's work, especially in the poems of this book. Thus "Spenser's Ireland" tells us that one is not free till he has been captured by belief; and "The Paper Nautilus" speaks of being "hindered to succeed." Miss Moore herself (in Whit Burnett, editor, *This Is My Best*, 1942) has spoken of "What Are Years?" as "elegiac," as a commentary upon the realization that even the most vigilant strugglers may lapse but that all may be "redeemed into inviolateness" by a sufficient courage.

In quite another context, yet similar in quality, are the values honored in "Rigorists," a poem remarking on the "reprieve" from starvation given to Eskimos in 1891 by a shipment of reindeer. These animals are examples of the "unconscious fastidiousness" Miss Moore praised in "Critics and Connoisseurs." Their adaptations to the rigors of their Lapland environment make them perfectly disciplined in body and spirit. Human artists may depict a decorative reindeer, but the real animal is itself a "queen of alpine flowers" and an "ornament" while at the same time a lion in strength. In this purposeful though unconscious beauty lay the promise of salvation for the Eskimo, a promise acted upon by the "quiet" educator Sheldon Jackson.

Miss Moore relied in "Rigorists" on extreme simplicity of form. The first six stanzas are presented as a quotation of a friend's description of the animals—a device, as in "Silence," that allows the poet to interpret descriptive details without seeming overly didactic. The last three stanzas then quietly marvel at the point that this creature of legend and ornament was in real life a savior. It is as though the reindeer is so good, even so obvious, an example of the beauty arising from purposeful strength that neither analysis nor commentary is necessary; the poet to make her point need only present useful details in an ordering as uncomplicated as the animal itself.

Advocacy of morally disciplined behavior, of rigorous adjustment to necessity, is not meant to deny the importance of freedom for the spirit. Celebration of this freedom is the theme of "Light Is Speech," a poem making traditional associations of France with frankness and of speech with the light of inspiration or spirit. The situation is that of the time of publication in early 1941. France had been conquered by the Nazis; the northern and western portions of the country were held by a German army of occupation, and the central and southern areas were ruled by a German-directed government at Vichy. "Speech" and "light" still reinforce each other, the first sentence assures us; they still are honorable when French in origin. The war, that is, has not erased the contributions of France to civilized man. We are to recall cocky Nazi threats, mentioned in a magazine article Miss Moore quotes later in the poem, that conquered nations would not be denied the blessings of illiteracy. Light still comes from the sun and the stars; it is in itself a "language," speaking to us of the values we associate with the name France. A lighthouse designed to be visible by both ships and planes is the symbolic descendant of such spokesmen for France as Voltaire, Montaigne, and the philologist Emile Littré.

The lighthouse is "defenceless," and Voltaire and Montaigne spoke out against odds. We English-speaking peoples, spared the invasion France has undergone, hear a spokesman for France demand, in character, that the truth be told even though it is unpleasant. The demand is quoted from Marshal Pétain, the soldier who had been a hero in World War I but in 1941 was regarded by the Free French and by the anti-Axis countries as a traitor because he was serving as head of the Vichy government. The ending, therefore, would appear to be ironic. In asserting that we can only reply that France means "enfranchisement," a country which will "'animate whoever thinks of her,'" the poem seems to be replying that France should stand not for the duplicity apparent at Vichy but for the values traditionally associated with her name.

France should have the courage to stand for values. The results and benefits of courage are subjects of the next three poems. "He 'Digesteth Harde Yron'" gives an example of the heroic which has survived barbarisms that killed others of its type. This is the "camel-sparrow" or ostrich. Rightly admired for his devotion to his young and for the value of even his plumes, this bird, the poem suggests, could hardly be expected to honor the men who in bygone days treacherously costumed themselves in his plumage in order to sneak up on and kill him. The contrast between the naturalness of an animal and the artificiality of men is similar to that drawn in "The Jerboa."

The next several lines, through the short sixth stanza, marvel over the ostrich's movements and the appropriateness of his role as a figure in legendry. (The *Collected Poems* printing omits two and a half stanzas which gave extra detail on the bird's methods of escape and his skill at running.) Stanza seven lists specific examples of waste, or worse. Yet the lavish but revolting banquet on ostrich brains and the ugly goblets referred to, indicate in a perverse way the human recognition of the justice and the genuineness the bird represents. They "dramatize a meaning" which is "always missed" by the man who sees only the misuse itself—the "externalist" who fails to see that unconcious respect for the bird causes man to choose it for his mistaken attention.

The power of the ostrich himself lies in his invisible spirit; even where there is no "freedom," his "so-called brute" courage knows this. The "heroism" the ostrich practiced to survive prevented the fate that overtook birds possessing more of "grandeur" but less of courage. His spirit, his courage of the invisible, has made the ostrich a creature capable of arousing respect and wonder. He is properly a symbol of justice, for by his courage he earned the survival he has achieved. Like the hero in "What Are Years?" who endured in his entrapment because he would not cower, the ostrich survives because he rebels against the "greed" that surrounds him: he feeds his spirit on the hard iron of his discouragements. The *Collected Poems* printing employs a seven-line stanza, compressing the material that in *What Are Years* took eight lines. As in "Virginia Britannia," the effect of compression is to slow the pace, making the poem seem more meditative.

One necessity for courage is understanding of one's circumstances. In "Smooth Gnarled Crape Myrtle" the scene is a tree, perhaps the artificial one of a floral display, or even a painted one. At any rate, it is properly stiff of leaf, rounded, and covered with flowers of pink and blue. That it is both smooth and gnarled makes it appropriate for the discoveries of paradox the poem is to make. Hopping about on the tree, seeming to be "askew" in this regularity, is a smooth, greenish bird, perhaps a female cardinal. The bird is "businesslike," apparently paying no heed to a companion. Between these two, weighting the twig which bears this "peculiar/bouquet," a male cardinal has lit. There should be here, the second stanza comments, some bird from legendry; the cardinal, in his fiery coloring and without the mate one expects him to have, looks out of place; he is a gnarl in the smooth scene.

He is also a disturber of intellectual complacencies. Sight of him, and of the female birds' detachment from him, calls to mind a sewing-box under which is a motto indicating that the conjunction of a pair of painted lovers is intended to illustrate friendship and love. But the picture and motto are a product of "artifice," always a bad quality in Miss Moore's opinion. Indeed, "Art is unfortunate": the picture and motto tell a lie. At least, they are not representative of the relationship between the male cardinal and the other birds in the crape myrtle tree.

Misunderstanding causes society at times to perceive an innocent bachelor to be a rake like a character in a Restoration drama. But the cardinal without a mate—"Rosalindless"—has come near other creatures without ulterior motives even though, ironically, he has lit on the myrtle which in some cultures has been a symbol of love. He has the hard wisdom that keeps him from assuming acceptance by others. The profundity of his comprehension is indicated by the remark that he does not sing but merely "says" what he knows, that he will cling to loneliness because without this feeling he would be more lonely still. Perhaps if he were to associate closely with others he would have to give up some of himself, be a less independent being, and thus be more truly lonely than he is in dignified isolation.

The cardinal's wisdom makes nonsense of the sentimental motto on the box; and it makes even more foolish the similar inscription recalled from an Elizabethan title page which avers that peace brings plenty and that wisdom brings peace. The last word in the poem, "Alas!", is the pet's comment on the folly of this pseudo-wisdom. It is a shame, she seems to say, that this is not so; but truth does not lie in such tidbits from the wishful thinking of self-deceiving humans. It is to be found in the hard knowledge expressed by the cardinal. He has the courage to accept the wisdom that says one must be wary of companionship. He may draw near to others, but he will not surrender himself to them.

The ostrich and the cardinal demonstrate that maturity requires acceptance of a "hard iron." That acknowledgment of responsibility for others makes necessary an equally stern discipline, is shown in "Bird-Witted." Three young mockingbirds seem large enough to care for themselves, but they still depend on their mother, even to the point that one who drops a morsel of food waits for the mother to pick it up for him. These young are indeed "bird-witted" in the usual meaning of the term— unable to care for themselves, too ignorant to recognize the danger of an approaching cat. The mother, however, is "bird-witted" in quite another sense. Accepting her duty to her young, and of necessity taking a serious view of life, she no longer sings the "delightful" notes of her pre-motherhood days; now that she is "astute," her voice has become "harsh."

Though without hope of reward for her effort, except that of continued toil to fill the hungry mouths of her young, the mother bird, made brave by sight of the intruding cat, swoops down and "half kills" him. The cat is "intellectual," he acts "cautiously"; his scheming is an example of the artifice scorned in "Smooth Gnarled Crape Myrtle." The mother bird, in contrast, acts out of an unconscious courage and self-discipline. Her behavior is prompted by maturity of spirit. The poem is faintly reminiscent of "The Frigate Pelican" in *Selected Poems,* but the pelicans were admirable for the adaptation to their environment which permitted them to save themselves from an approaching python; in "Bird-Witted" the admiration is for courageous action on behalf of others. The contrast is indicative of the difference between the first and middle periods of Miss Moore's work.

Ostrich, cardinal, and mockingbird all exemplify the maturity which is the reward of courage. Part of the answer to the query "what are years?" seems to be that they are an opportunity for the individual of armor and restraint to develop a wisdom that will enable him to comprehend and even to grow strong on the hard iron life will offer him.

The three poems centered on birds dealt with the behavior of representative heroic individuals. The nature of whole societies over considerable periods of time is taken up in the next two poems. Both "Virginia Britannia" and "Spenser's Ireland" are excellent examples of Miss Moore's mature use of descriptive poetry to convey commentary on ethics. "Virginia Britannia" explores the connections among the Virginia country-side, the Indians, and the early white settlers. Combining straight-forward statement with humor and indignation, the poem speculates on the presence in this environment of foolish and at times wicked human actions, as well as of amusing if misguided aspirations. Its assertions are direct, but are so carefully embedded in details that they seem a part of the poem's texture. Half of the tenth stanza, for example, is a statement that man in Virginia has lacked "mercy." But the reader has been so thoroughly prepared by illustrations implying this point that the comment seems not an intrusion but an inevitable recognition of fact. The poem is concentrated and fresh in syntax without being abrupt. The *Collected Poems* version compresses into twelve-line and thirteen-line stanzas material that in the *What Are Years* printing took seventeen lines; as in "He 'Digesteth Harde Yron,'" the change is an improvement, the compactness slowing the pace to match the thoughtfulness of the content. The reader, incidentally, will notice that the crape myrtle, ostrich, cardinal, and mockingbird of the three poems preceding this one all reappear in it.

After detailing some of the Old Dominion scene, Miss Moore mentions a few of the evidences of early settlement that remain. These include the remark on a settler's tombstone that "a great sinner lyeth here," a thought that is quaint in effect at this point, but is suggestive of the poem's attitude toward the history of Virginia's colonization. The man who would admit to sin was "unusual," we are told. Thought of this brings up the incongruity of Captain John Smith's company as well as of some of the early Indians. The careful formality the English on one occasion employed in crowning an Indian chief suggests the care which has produced in "unEnglish" Virginia luxuriant growths of the wall rose and the yew.

But neither Indian nor settler represents the true spirit of the land. The fourth stanza calls on us to observe "the terse Virginian," the mockingbird that here is a creature of mettle who can adopt the guise of any native bird or with insouciance dominate an English garden pedestal. The suggestion seems to be that the bird is the true life of Virginia, that in a guarded defiance he frequents man's habitations, watching with a self-assurance born of his knowledge that he is the permanent heir of the land. The bird is seen sitting in the garden of a country home, perhaps in Williamsburg. Pansies that bloom there in splendid but short-lived pride are, it is implied, an emblem of all ante-bellum Virginia where settlers in "establishing the Negro"—as a slave, we recall—were importing an "inadvertent ally," an enemy of tyranny. Settlers who were as odd as the Indians they conquered; Negroes who were to help overcome the social system which had imprisoned them—Virginia has been, indeed, an "inconsistent flower-bed." Some of the oddities, some of the paradoxes in Virginia floriculture illustrate the point; and these are paralleled by half-amusing, half-puzzling comparisons between an Indian princess and an English girl and by the intermixture even yet of Indian and English names.

Mention of aristocratic names given to frontier counties recalls the contrasting "tactless" defiance of an early American patriot flag; this contrast brings to mind such oddities as the combination of "cotton-mouth snakes and cotton-fields," and the "serpentine" shape of a beautiful wall. Such incongruities are emblematic of the state's history. There has been, it is now asserted, some cruelty in all "our" efforts—all the exploration, imperialism, and colonizing of Europe-born civilization. Mercy has not been a leading characteristic of "us." And the Indian, despite his fearsome reputation, was not all cruelty. Realization that the vaunted white civilization was frequently cruel, the condemned Indian society often magnanimous, is associated with the paradox that the supposed luxuries of the civilized settlers were "stark" in comparison with the attributes Virginia already had—the seemingly drab hedge-sparrow, for example, which sings in "ardour" his "ecstatic" joy. Miss Moore humorously specifies in the eleventh stanza, and verifies in her notes to the poem, the point that this remarkable avis "wakes up seven minutes sooner than the lark."

The touch of humor is purposeful, for the poem is not to turn into a defense of Indians and an attack on whites. Native and English flora have by now become indistinguishable, the last stanza tells us; there is no longer any point in dwelling upon whatever differences may once have existed. Over all the scene and over the continuing assertiveness of the Virginia town—whose inhabitants, we may assume, include whites, Negroes, and whatever Indians survive—the clouds expand to dwarf the "arrogance" of mankind, the pride that prevented men from seeing the possibilities Virginia has offered. By their grandeur and their suggestion that other possibilities await man's discovery, the clouds give an "intimation of what glory is." The theme of despoliation, at least of failure to see the true possibilities of a land, links the poem to "The Plumet Basilisk" and to "The Jerboa."

Quite another kind of failure to develop possibilities is examined in "Spenser's Ireland." This poem muses half humorously about the obduracy remarked upon in Spenser's "A View of the State of Ireland," a stubbornness Miss Moore's poem finds still to be observed in Ireland. The characters in Spenser's dialogue were puzzled by Irish refusal to submit even to laws which, at least in the view of the conquering English, were intended for their own peace and good order. Miss Moore somewhat similarly views the Irish as examples of those who fail to see that freedom comes only with discipline and belief, the wisdom she asserts in this volume in both "What Are Years?" and "The Paper Nautilus."

Though "Spenser's Ireland" talks of customs now abandoned, it deliberately uses present-tense verbs to suggest that the spirit of obduracy with which these behaviors were associated in the times of Spenser still exists. Thus the poem says that the Irish are "natural"—an adjective having, it seems, both the modern meaning "undisciplined" and the Shakespearian (and Spenserian) sense "foolish." By way of illustrating this, the poem mentions the cloak or mantle with its long, useless sleeves which Spenser's observers found distasteful in the sixteenth century (they believed it was a hiding place for lawbreakers). The idea surely is not to say that the Irish today garb themselves in mantles, but rather to intimate that the spirit which once made them cling to the garment despite English objections is still alive.

The poem opens with lines which present the characteristics summed up in the word "natural." Unchanging Ireland is kind;

but it is also "green," this adjective perhaps referring both to the colors of the land and to the immaturity of its inhabitants. The Irish respond neither to scoldings nor to blows, but are easily hurt if not spoken to; they are, indeed, scarcely adult. The second stanza remarks on the legend that, to charm away supernatural intruders, the Irish play the harp backwards and that, to attain invisibility and thus elude giants, they swallow fern seed. Might there not be, it asks, some magical device for unlearning obduracy and thus restoring the "enchantment" of an Ireland unspoiled by the stubbornness of its people? Representative of Irish pig-headedness are the grandmothers who appear in place of mothers in Irish stories of "hindered" characters: the distant past rules Irish life.

Whoever maintains so rigorous an attitude fails to see that freedom—of spirit, we gather—comes only to the person who is the "captive" of "supreme belief," to the man who, we may paraphrase, has the discipline of attitude and behavior which Miss Moore thinks belief affords. This trust in the necessity and virtue of faith is not "credulity," the poem continues. The devotee of sport fishing who is a craftsman at tying flies has the pride which rightfully comes from such care: he is not a victim of "madness," at least not insofar as his pride is owing to his skill. (By alluding to the art of fly-tying Miss Moore has picked an apt modern parallel to the magical crafts of earlier centuries). Hands of those who agree that accuracy of performance is valuable produce the leather-like Irish damask which is so fine as to be watertight. But less carefully crafted art—the poem mentions jewelry that is illustrated in a *National Geographic* magazine article referred to in the notes—is not so beautiful as the bloom of the fuchsia, a product of Irish nature.

Spenser's characters speculated on whether the stubbornness of the Irish arose from something in the stars or in the soil. Miss Moore similarly speculates on whether the idea of Eire—an independent Ireland—and the birds which seem to represent the spirit of the country indicate an inextricable pig-headedness in the nature of Ireland. If so, she asserts, let them be like Gerald, eleventh Earl of Kildare, who according to Irish horror stories changed himself into various animal forms—let them, that is, be transformed into something else. And then, like one of the Irish enchanters of old, she wishes away these indications of Irish perversity.

Yet the poem must close on a half ironic, half humorous note, for Miss Moore is aware of her own distant Irish ancestry. She wishes she could believe the sentimental assurance of the *National Geographic* writer that the Irish will share one another's troubles, for she, herself Irish, is "dissatisfied." Ireland is still, it would appear, that land of unending resistance which troubled Spenser. The poem's warning and its chiding of the Irish, we may take it, are really directed at the refusal of stubborn men everywhere to recognize the need for the discipline Miss Moore thinks belief can give. The poem's presentation of the errors in stubbornness is the counterpart, of course, of the praise she gave Irish fortitude in "Sojourn in the Whale."

To see that the accuracy afforded by repetition is an object of Miss Moore's practice, we need only observe how she repeats her carefully patterned stanza forms throughout a poem. It is not surprising to find her basing a poem—"Four Quartz Crystal Clocks"—on a report that four quartz vibrators kept at even temperature independently maintain the same time and thus provide a standard against which clocks may be checked. Nor is it surprising to find her mentioning that these furnish accurate time for the media of communication, the channels which should convey truth. We know, she remarks, such a historical truth as the fact that Napoleon is dead; and we also know such a scientific truth as the fact that the vibrations of quartz prisms will vary if the temperature changes.

The conjunction of the historical and the scientific seems to suggest that Miss Moore sees one order of time and truth. Thought of the "repetition" of temperature suggests the "accuracy" which should characterize the procedure of the scientist. In a technique similar to that she employed in "Virginia Britannia," Miss Moore now darts back to her store of examples of the quality she would illustrate, rather than giving a rationalistic analysis of it. One can "see," she remarks, that an aye-aye is not a potto, that a bell-boy is not a buoy-ball (she says parenthetically that he should not let himself be embarrassed by punning remarks on the similarity in names), and that glass eyes are not eyeglasses. Even such repetitions should contribute not to confusion but to accuracy, she says. There is a wink in her eye, of course, for in her punning she is taking advantage of possible confusions.

And "you realize," she says in her tone of pleasant reasonableness, that, when you hear the telephone company time announcement (dialed, significantly, by means of a repetitious number), what you are hearing is Jupiter praising "punctuality." The reference to Jupiter perhaps is intended to allude to his identification in myth as the spirit of air, for it is air that is vibrated to produce the sound we hear. In a rather complicated piece of punning etymology, Miss Moore also suggests that the name Jupiter is derived from the French "jour" for day and the Latin "pater" for father. At any rate, Jupiter functions as the god of day and is said to be the son of Father Time, of that Chronos who once ate most of his other children (all but air, water, and the grave, these being three which time cannot devour). Jupiter as the air, the message from the vibrating quartz prisms, is thus telling Father Time himself that punctuality "is not a crime," but is in fact a virtue. This conclusion in which the action turns back upon itself is, of course, apt evidence of the ability of repetition to insist upon meaning. The last line as it appeared in the poem's original printing in 1940 read "is not now a crime." The "now" seemed to suggest a limit to the time during which accuracy has been valued; omitting it, as *Collected Poems* does, makes it possible to think of accuracy as a permanent value.

Miss Moore also employs the descriptive mode in "The Pangolin," her fullest statement on relationships among the animal, human, and spiritual kingdoms. Despite the humorous recognition of her own affection for such creatures as the pangolin in the exclamation "Another armoured animal," Miss Moore's real subject is the nature of man, that animal for whom no physical armoring is adequate. The pangolin, indeed, represents the perfection of the courage and restraint Miss Moore values; he has the "unconscious fastidiousness" praised in "Critics and Connoisseurs" and the naturalness admired in "The Jerboa." But, as "Melanchthon" and "When I Buy Pictures" indicated, something more than these qualities is needed. "The Pangolin" shows that the something more is grace, an inspiration from a spiritual world. The poem also gives Miss Moore's fullest statement on man himself. It finds him half comical, half contemptible, and yet treats him warmly because, though he lacks the perfection of the animal, he has greater possibility.

Of the poem's nine stanzas, the first five are devoted to an appreciative detailing of the pangolin's characteristics; the last four cautiously compare and contrast man with these. The careful presentation of the animal's armoring and strategems gives concrete ground for the delight expressed in him; it also provides a listing of features useful for the parallelism with man. Continuing the admiration of repetition given in "Four Quartz Crystal Clocks," the poem celebrates the repetition of pattern in the pangolin's scales. Occasionally it matches such repetition in its own style. Thus a list of elements the pangolin may exclude from his nest is given as a series of nouns linked by "and" rather than by punctuation; the sculptures on a cathedral are said to include "monk and monk and monk"; and the last stanza describes the succession of days as "new and new and new." Those with an interest in style should note the various changes in wording and punctuation in the different printed versions of the poem.

The pangolin—the scaly anteater of Africa and Asia—is, we are told, wonderfully made; like Leonardo da Vinci, he is both artist and engineer. Armor seems unnecessary on so finely wrought a creature; yet, considering that he at times becomes covered with ants, it is good that he is so securely fashioned that he can make even his eyes impenetrable. When endangered, he does not fight; but, with the grace of Westminster Abbey ironwork—an allusion that introduces an association of grace and cathedrals to be developed in later stanzas—he withdraws or rolls himself into a ball. Even this is not the limit of his resources for security, for he has "sting-proof scales" and he can retreat into a rock-lined nest. Indeed, he has developed a virtually absolute restraint; he can shut out "Sun and moon and day and night and man and beast"—elements and considerations which man "in all his vileness" does not have the power to exclude. Each of these has a "splendour," an "excellence"; mention that the animal can escape them but that man cannot, suggests the theme which is soon to become apparent: the animal though admirable in himself is, after all, limited; man, being more greatly gifted, also faces, and must accept, greater responsibilities and challenges. Perfection of restraint is not an ethical goal for a human being.

The pangolin is in his own element a creature filled with fear, yet fearsome in his turn. More elaboration upon the marvels of his protective stratagems leads to the thought of what in *Collected Poems* is described as his "not unchain-like machine-like/form." In *A Marianne Moore Reader* (1961) the wording is "measured/tread of the machine," an alteration avoiding awkwardness but also changing the emphasis from his form to his manner of motion. The new wording is appropriate, for thought of the pangolin's movement brings up again the matter of his physical grace. From that it is an easy transition in the sixth stanza to a consideration of grace as evidenced in some of man's works. Since Miss Moore chooses to illustrate this quality by remarking upon the artistry of cathedrals, the reader is carried quickly into a meditation upon spiritual grace. In a few lines the poem has moved from the physical to the esthetic and thence to the spiritual.

The pangolin developed his delightful gracefulness because of the adaptation of his form to his functions; he is designed to successfully meet "adversities, conversities." To explain grace, we are told, requires "a curious hand." We are then given what is indeed a curious, though appropriate, working out of the idea: if it were not for the fact of immortality, the poem asks, would the engineer-artists who built great cathedrals have "slaved" to associate representations of grace with illustrations—so to speak— of kindliness, of long-enduring time, and of sin being cured? Because these men who were representatives of the central culture of their time had faith in immortality, they could believe in the idea of a grace which incorporated these concepts. Their belief made itself evident in their art, with its rows of grave monks and its graceful mullions. To find grace in a human construction is not unusual, it is suggested; for a sailboat, an example of gracefulness, was man's "first machine."

Like the sailboat, the pangolin moves quietly and is a model of "exactness"; thought of his occasional human-like "postures" brings the poem back again to man. Less well, if less narrowly, adapted to his functions, man misses half of what he sets out to find; he is complex, embodying in one being a variety of functions that in the animal kingdom are distributed among many creatures. Though, or because, he is relatively infinite in capacity —he may, for example, appear in any stage of dress from the "bedizened" to "stark" nudity—man is as yet far from the perfection achieved by creatures whose possibilities are more limited. Thus man, the "writing-master," the self-conscious intelligence of this world, claws out (as might a griffon, a fabulous monster) such quasi-philosophical crypticisms as "Like does not like like that is obnoxious," and misspells the word "error" itself. One must keep a sense of humor when considering such an animal. Though "unignorant," having the gift of a certain intelligence and self-knowledge, man fails in his attempt to pose as unemotional because he is "all emotion." There is hope for him because he has "power to grow," but in his present stage one had best be wary of him.

The pangolin, not being self-conscious, is fearful or fearsome as instinct directs; man, being aware of self, is either boastfully unafraid or a coward. A mammal, not so separate from the pangolin as he might like to think, man retreats like an animal to his abode. But it is no secure pangolin nest, for manufactured habiliments are his only armor. Night is the pangolin's time of greatest activity; but man, in some ways a counterpart of the animal, is "thwarted by the dusk"—darkness for him, we may deduce, being a depression of spirit. The animal accepts calmly the days and nights as they come to him; man, the creature of less perfection but more diversity, finds that each return of day is a new emotional experience. He never learns that naturalness of attitude which, inborn in the animal, enables it to function without some of the fears and foolishness that afflict man himself. Yet in the possibility of renewal, the fact of diversity, lies hope for this imperfect creature, man. This renewal comes with each sunrise, for each day brings a resurrection and a possibility of new grace. The man of this poem is the man of "What Are Years?": he is defeated, but he goes on trying.

The leading issue for *What Are Years* is indicated by its title poem's consideration of the elements in heroic behavior. That poem and the succeeding ones present these elements as courage, self-discipline based on belief, such esthetic values as craftsmanship and accuracy, and the need for grace. What secures and fortifies all these as well as associated requirements is suggested in "The Paper Nautilus," the closing poem, which asserts that "love" is "the only fortress/strong enough to trust to."

The female of the paper nautilus, a mollusk related to the squid and the octopus, raises its young carefully in a thin, glasslike shell. The poem opens with assertions that she does not exercise this care for commercial reasons, nor for the delight of inobservant writers (we may suspect a sarcastic dig at the easy moralizing of Oliver Wendell Holmes's famed "The Chambered Nautilus"). This "perishable" shell is a "souvenir of hope" because it houses the eggs; the nautilus guards it by cradling it in her eight arms. A complicated parallel now first remarks that Hercules in his struggle with the hydra found that his strength was renewed by anger when he was bitten by Cancer, the crab and one of the hydra's supporters; it then implies that, in a similar paradox, the nautilus and its shell become free when the new-hatched young they have guarded struggle free from their supervision. The success of the hatching makes it appear that the guarding arms of the nautilus had intelligence, that they knew the singular value of love as "the only fortress." Perhaps the nautilus is only a creature of instinct, but its behavior nevertheless provides a lesson for man.

The ethical presentation of the poem arises with a seemingly casual grace out of a citation of exact details of the subject, rather than by the easy and obvious analogy that Holmes used. The result is a fine demonstration of how a poem may convey a statement without surrendering its being to didacticism.

II *Nevertheless: Be Wary*

Miss Moore's next volume, an even slimmer one, brought together in 1944 under the title *Nevertheless* six poems originally published in magazines in the early 1940's. The title seems to indicate that these pieces qualify the assertions of *What Are Years*. Since most of them repeat Miss Moore's usual emphases on courage, craftsmanship, and honesty toward oneself, we may deduce that, though in *What Are Years* Miss Moore gives primary value to grace and love, she does not want her reader to think she is concerned only with such ultimates: in daily life courage and the values associated with it remain the immediate necessities.

First in order is the poem labeled on original publication "It Is Late, I Can Wait" but now titled "Nevertheless." It seems in particular a continuation, almost a qualification, of the assertion in "The Paper Nautilus" that love is the only trustworthy fortress. Nevertheless, this poem seems to say, courage is primary for survival. The poem presents a series of examples of courageous behavior in the face of great difficulty: the strawberry that manages to appear a work of art even when torn open; the apple-seeds that are neatly patterned, though locked in place; the roots of the dandelion rubber plant that survive in frozen ground; the prickly pear leaf that, though caught on barbed wire, sends a shoot down to earth. All these, we note, are examples of victory within captivity; like Hercules in "The Paper Nautilus," they may be described as "hindered to succeed." They serve as examples from the plant world of the possibility of winning survival despite, even because of, captivity—the possibility which on the level of ideas is cited in "Spenser's Ireland" and "What Are Years?"

These examples of heroic behavior demonstrate the need for resolute action: they show that "Victory won't come/to me unless I go/to it." As usual in Miss Moore's work, this message—if we may term it that—is not elaborated upon by methods of prose analysis and explication; instead, it is followed immediately by yet another example of courageous endeavor: the grape tendril, which by knotting and reknotting, chokes an intruding twig. By means of courage, indeed, the weak can overcome his feebleness; the strong can master himself. The poem ends with a final example of "fortitude": the cherry stem that, despite its fragility, has conveyed to the fruit the necessary sap. The "love" cited in "The Paper Nautilus" as the ultimate value is of course an ideal; but the importance of courage is "nevertheless" not to be forgotten.

The determined, indeed, are the best associates, or so "The Wood-Weasel" tells us. At least, this is true of those who, like the creature of the title, have a sense of humor in their situation. There is humor in the poem's opening remark that the creature "emerges daintily," a remark which postpones mention of the animal's common designation, skunk. We are told that he is both black and white, that he wears "goat-fur," and that he is "wood-warden"—all details which suggest some association of the humble skunk with Pan, lord of woods and animals. In his white-black wool—repeated emphasis on the colors of his coat seems to reinforce the suggestion of resemblance to Pan, the goat-man—he is truly the "totem," the symbol of determination. Though considered an outlaw, he conducts himself as a chief; and he is capable of any required self-defense. Yet he is "playful." He is, indeed, an altogether admirable model. (When published in *Nevertheless* the first four letters of "Wood-weasels" in the last line were printed in capitals, suggesting a contrast with the ordinary weasel of ill repute; in *Collected Poems* Miss Moore prints "Wood . . . ," evidently having decided the contrast was obvious enough without the emphasis.)

Fortitude and determination are two of the qualities of wisdom. "Elephants" is another of Miss Moore's poems in which the well-defended exemplify wisdom. The poem opens with a scene of two elephant trunks locked in a wrestling match. Since the forces are equal, the picture is almost a still-life; it is an emblem of that unity, that blending of what are in some aspects the opposed, which is one theme of the poem. The elephants, we are told, are not fighting seriously; their match is something of "a pastime." Stanzas three through six present another instance of a unity of seeming opposites: the picture of a mahout sleeping cradled in the hollow of his sleeping elephant's body. The elephant is "unconscious" of the man's weight, and the man's pose indicates he feels as secure as though he were himself an elephant. Like the wrestling elephants of the opening stanzas, the two creatures, beast and man, seem one.

What is said of elephants in the rest of the poem, we gather, may be applied to man. Yet, as "The Pangolin" shows, Miss Moore knows that animal and man are not one, even though the appearance is "as if" they were. Because truth doesn't permit the identification the poet would like to make, because all man's interpretations are "as ifs," she exclaims that "we are at/much unease." Man does not have the security he would like, physical or mental; the magical attainment of "serenity" is a "master-piece" achieved only by the elephant.

The last ten stanzas investigate the nature of this achievement. The elephants are not really participants in man's activities. Ceylonese elephants are "templars of the Tooth," guardians of the tooth-relic of Buddha in Kandy. But their attitude is of "revery not reverence"—in religious ceremonies they walk in a thoughtful mood, not resisting what they cannot hope to defeat, but not giving up their independence. Yet in the naturalness of their behavior the parading elephants form what is in itself a "religious procession." Blessed by the sacred tooth they guard, the beasts in turn bless the street they line as they watch the passage of the sacred white elephant that carries the tooth-relic itself.

Though acceding to the directions of gnat-like men, the mighty white elephant belies his skin; white, we are told, is "the colour of worship and of mourning," but the elephant does not take part in human culture and is "too wise" to lament the loss of his own way of life. He is, like many of Miss Moore's favorite creatures, "a life prisoner but reconciled." The elephant, subjected to the proddings of the mahout, is a captive who has developed the wisdom to accept with grace what he cannot prevent. Though, when first captured, he resisted till forced to curl his trunk in defeat, he has straightened his trunk now: he has learned "reason" and has "revived," has determined to live in dignity under the conditions imposed on him. The captive elephant, like man, lives in a world he did not make, did not ask for, and does not consider ideal; but he makes the best of it and, in his wisdom, sets an example for man.

Wise in his sphere as Socrates was in his, the elephant "tinctures" his "gravity" with "sweetness." He permits "man the encroacher" to make use of him; and, in accepting courteously the wishes of his conqueror, he sets an example of "brotherhood" and thus of true knowledge. He reminds us by his action of the Sanskrit verb for knowing, "bud" (related to the name "Buddha," the enlightened one). At this point, after the first two words of what is now the next-to-last stanza, the printing of the poem in *Nevertheless* had approximately eight lines citing specific detail to show that elephants do not after all have the magical powers of Buddha—they cannot "alter their shape, bisect hairs in the dark." This passage did not further the movement of the poem, and Miss Moore obviously decided when preparing *Collected Poems* that its content was not necessary.

These "knowers," the elephants, inspire the idea that they are "allied to man" and indeed that they could "change roles with" him. Reassertion of this idea indicates that we are to take the remaining six lines of the poem as applying not so much to the elephant as to man himself. "Hardship makes the soldier," we are told: fortitude, we may paraphrase, is developed through hard experience. "Teachableness," willingness to learn, then makes man into a "philosopher" who realizes that wisdom lies in being, like the elephant, modest about one's knowledge, in willingness to concede that one cannot be "sure that he knows." One necessity for serenity, that is, is willingness to live with uncertainty: to think in the "as ifs" of the sixth stanza may put us "at much unease," but it is the only possibility for the perceptive man. Who "rides on a tiger" cannot get off: he who takes the tiger as his model for behavior can never be anything other than a tiger himself. But he who relies on the elephant will develop the wisdom that brings serenity.

The elephant's survival, despite his captivity, is a product of courage; he meets the prescription for heroic behavior outlined in such poems as "What Are Years?" and "He 'Digesteth Harde Yron.'" But courage can lead to more than physical survival amid difficulties, even to more than survival of spirit. In "Elephants" Miss Moore is saying that it can lead as well to a profound wisdom—to an acceptance, which though guarded, is not merely passive or resistant. It can lead, that is, to that spiritual victory over "mortality" that is best named "serenity."

That "inner happiness," a quality akin to serenity, can produce a forthright craftsmanship resulting in art is demonstrated in "A Carriage from Sweden." There is in a Brooklyn museum, the poem remarks, a "country cart" from Sweden so finely made that its very presence, even though it is not at the moment on display, makes one feel at home "in this city of freckled/integrity." In its honest workmanship the cart recalls the days of Gustavus Adolphus and George Washington, days when character was not commonly "freckled." Reference to Sweden as having "once" been opposed to compromise may be a jibe at Swedish accomodation to Nazi demands during World War II, or it may be simply a suggestion that Sweden shares a general decline in integrity. In any case half a dozen stanzas exclaim over the artful construction and decoration of the carriage and the Scandinavian virtues of which it is reminiscent. These considerations lead, naturally enough, to speculation on the probable source for such spirited integrity, for a product and a people "responsive and/responsible." The answer of the last seven lines is that the source is not Sweden's topography or geology but the Swedes' combination of genuineness and imagination; it is also their ethic that values beauty, skill, and integrity. In striving to meet this stalwart ideal, the Swedes inevitably produce a work of art. The last seven lines contain a succession of "s" sounds, a series of sibilants perhaps intended to reinforce the association of Sweden with the sturdy and the skilled.

Although simplicity makes for art in "A Carriage from Sweden," there are other values than simplicity. The enchantment of complexity, of multitudinous inconsistencies, is hailed in "The Mind Is an Enchanting Thing." The paradox is that the mind enchants and is in turn enchanted. Opening remarks that the mind has the beauties of a varicolored insect wing suggest the thought that, like the kiwi or apteryx (the long-beaked, hair-feathered bird of New Zealand), the mind "walks along with its eyes on the ground": it does not need the help of sensory organs to see where it is going. It need not hear what is said, for it has the "ear" of memory; a few lines later it is the "eye" of memory—it perceives what memory wishes interpreted.

The mind is, indeed, worthy of celebration because it is "trued by regnant certainty." It, that is, has its sources in a sphere beyond this one. Thus given a fundamental stability, it can not only perceive veiled truths and remove "dejection"; it can also shimmer in an aura of iridescence and accommodate without disturbance the "inconsistencies" of a baroque composer. Being itself the height of "unconfusion," it willingly "submits" to tests of the validity of any "confusion" which may seem to appear in its understanding. It is, in short, neither a weak, unstable power easily baffled by paradox and uncertainty, nor an absolute, unchanging certitude that would, like Herod, persist in a ruthless course. Like the serene creature of "Elephants," the mind can live with and grow strong on "as ifs." It is, we gather, because of its spiritual connections both beautiful and true.

The earlier poem "In the Days of Prismatic Colour" emphasized the errors of an undue sophistication; its attitudes are reinforced, not contradicted, in "The Mind Is an Enchanting Thing" because what this poem values is not sophisticated murkiness but acceptance of the inevitable confusions of experience. "Melanchthon," after all, told us that there is at the core of the self a "Beautiful element of unreason." "The Mind Is an Enchanting Thing" says that awareness of the self's connection with spirit will enable one to accept "unreason" with serenity.

One is not, of course, to be so enchanted by his own mind that he armors himself against all feeling for others. "The Paper Nautilus" uses the military metaphor "the only fortress" to describe love. *Nevertheless* ends with "In Distrust of Merits," a poetic investigation of World War II's demonstration of the need for love in human relationships. The poem incorporates considerations of the courage, armoring, guilt, and beauty that are frequent topics in Miss Moore's work.

"In Distrust of Merits" opens with the question whether soldiers—the Allies of World War II—have been "Strengthened" only to achieve martial "merits." The answer is that they are fighting not for merely military objectives but to put down the "blind" who cannot see that enslavement of others is also enslavement of self. Like a litany, the next lines with their prominent "o" sounds appeal to a "star," perhaps of knowledge or truth, and to a tumultuous ocean, perhaps the world that by its disturbance is teaching us "depth." The exclamation "Lost at sea before they fought!" seems less a lament for some actual event than a cry aroused by the thought that we are "lost" because of our own deficiencies before we can even enter a struggle for truth.

A more direct appeal calls on symbols of Judaism, Christianity, and Ethiopia to be "joined." Ethiopia seems to represent the colored races of mankind; and we may note that in Miss Moore's poem, "Leonardo da Vinci's," Ethiopia is the country of the lion that is emblematic of Christ's resurrection. The alternatives we face are hate, that breeds death; and love, that brings kingship and even saintliness. As the beasts of "Elephants" blessed by their worthiness the symbol they guarded, so here trust is said to breed trust.

In the third stanza the assertion becomes specific: the soldiers are fighting that "I," any one of us, may be cured of the disease "My/Self." Their action is an atonement for our sin (a point elaborated upon in "Keeping Their World Large," where the soldiers' sacrifice is said to equal a rebirth of the spirit of Christ). In egocentrism we become self-cannibalistic: no enemy could so harm us. A man who is only physically blind can, if necessary, be escaped; but, we are reminded, Job discovered long ago that a man given the capacity to perceive who refuses to use this capacity rightly—a stubborn self—cannot be so easily evaded. All the unseeing and "arrogant" are now again admonished that trust, such trust as that accompanying love for one another, brings "power."

Therefore "We"—the plural contrasts with the "I" of self-centeredness—are declared to vow that we will never hate men no matter what skin color or creed they may have. Brotherhood of man was one of the fixed values celebrated in "The Labours of Hercules"; its difficulty of achievement again is recognized in this passage of "In Distrust of Merits" with the remark that we are "not competent" to vow it. The soldiers are the ones undergoing risk to make brotherhood effective; their heroism is what "cures me"—unless, the question occurs, "I" am "what/ I can't believe in." The "I," that is, may after all be closer to the enemy than it cares to realize: it may itself harbor hatred.

Soldiers would, if struggling in anger or in hatred, be moved only by "outside" things, by merely human forces. But, when armored with patience, soldiers fight well and even in a kind of ethical beauty because, we gather, they then are responding to what Miss Moore might term inside things, promptings of the spirit. As long as men act without acknowledging spirit, the world will be only a home for orphans, a desolation where peace will not come without sorrow. Yet the agonies of war will not be wasted if they "teach us how to live," to discover our spiritual sources.

The final appeal is to the "hate-hardened" heart of the self—the heart that, because it does not recognize its sources, will become rust. What this heart, this self, must see is that never was there "a war that was/not inward." The roots of war ultimately are not exterior to the individual; they lie within the self, in its failures to behave ethically. One who—like "I"—did nothing to forestall World War II, who has done nothing to rid himself of hate and to open his eyes to love, commits a treachery to the self. He must see that man, the dust of the earth, and his hatreds are only temporary; but the "Beauty" of brotherhood and of the spirit is "everlasting." Soldiers can conquer only the exterior enemy. Each of us must vanquish within himself the error that is the source of the world's agonies.

The poem is in the form of a confession, almost of what in Elizabethan times was called a "complaint." Though it deals with a vast social upheaval, it is not "social poetry" but an energetic consideration of the contributions of the individual self to chaos. By this point in her career Miss Moore, though still honoring independence of mind, was no longer advocating the kind of armoring symbolized by the cliff in "The Fish"—the aloof, almost suspicious restraint from contact with others. Yet in urging brotherhood she was still honoring individualism, for she saw brotherhood as a function of the individual heart.

Of all Miss Moore's verse, probably only "Poetry" is better known than "In Distrust of Merits." According to A Marianne Moore Reader, when asked by Donald Hall for her opinion on the poem, she said she likes it for what she sees as the sincerity in it, but thinks it lacking in form; it is, she told him, "just a protest—disjointed, exclamatory." The poem did offend one usually enthusiastic critic, Randall Jarell, who is reported in the introduction to Selden Rodman's 100 Modern Poems as scorning what he saw as its message that man may be taught to live by the sufferings of war. It may be replied that lessonings are not always pleasant and that in any case the sufferings of war function in this poem as object lessons, as what the educationists call "audio-visual aids," rather than as matters of philosophical import in themselves. The poem is something of a companion piece to the later "Keeping Their World Large"; the reader interested in further comparisons should also read two uncollected war poems: the not entirely clear "You Say You Said" (1918) and the speculative considerations of courage in "We Call Them the Brave" (1951).

III *Uncollected: The Self Reviewed*

Collected Poems ends with a "Hitherto Uncollected" section of nine poems that had appeared in magazines since publication of *Nevertheless* (1944). The first five poems consider qualities the individual should have, the stance he should maintain in the universe in which he finds himself, and particularly how he may achieve the stability amid confusion that was honored in "The Mind Is an Enchanting Thing." In "A Face" the speaker, looking in a mirror, not only sees no sign of various unpleasant character traits but also sees no indication of what her real nature might be. This inability to decipher self is perhaps "no real impasse"; yet it angers the person who considers how simple the requirements for good character are: could there not be detected, she exclaims, those qualities of "ardour" and curiosity which "are all one needs to be!" The unusual grammar of this clause is intended to suggest that the desired qualities are not mere coatings or appendages but integral to the self. In contrast to the blankness the speaker sees is the memory of a few faces that remain "a delight," faces that, we deduce, showed their owners' possession of the admired qualities. The exclamatory tone of some lines and a mention of "desperation" do not make this bitter or sarcastic self-depreciation; rather, the effect is of ironic humor. Is there any among us who has not in his candid moments been distressed by the revelations of the mirror?

Although the mirror arouses one kind of meditation on perfections, another kind is suggested by thought of the beings whose nature is the subject of "By Disposition of Angels." The poem opens with hypotheses about them, asking for explanation of their supposed function as messengers, suggesting that they may represent a "steadfastness" made clear by its contrast with the mystery surrounding it, and asking if they may not best be "heard" by an auditor who is perhaps at some remove from them. Angels are "unparticularities," perhaps creatures not confined to a self. They are indeed characterized by a "steadiness" heightened by its inaccessibility, just as the apparent brightness of a star is increased in a dark sky.

The angel is like a star, a fir, or speech that is indifferent to a human observer: thus the mysterious is comparable only to and is explained only by other mysteries. Yet this, we gather, makes the angel only the more interesting; "live and elate," it exists in an incomparability which obviates any "need" on our part either to draw analogies between it and people we know or to make judgments of it. It is a perfect or an ideal being which says by its existence all that need be said. We may speculate that it represents the ideal poem, and that it is to be associated with the independent behavior Miss Moore admires. But the poem fittingly gives no obvious clues for interpretations.

Integrity obviously is a chief quality of angels, but that it is a quality we humans have yet to achieve is made apparent in "The Icosasphere," a poem inspired, as the notes explain, by accounts of an engineer's successful development of an economical method for certain utilizations of steel by study of a twenty-faced sphere. Integration of creature and function is demonstrated in the world of nature, the first stanza tells us: nesting in the "merged green density," the unified world of flora, birds unconsciously accomplish mathematical regularities that are "feats of rare efficiency." But man, lacking the perfected adjustment of animal life, displays such horrifying behavior as that found in the selfish competition of thousands of people for an inheritance to which few had a just claim. Yet man also is capable of developing the admirable icosahedron. The men who could design that might well be asked to tell us, the poem concludes, how the ancient Egyptians raised their tall granite slabs without machinery. We may take this as a wish that all of us might more easily accomplish integration of desire and action. As in "Rigorists," the approach in "The Icosasphere" is similar to that of light verse. Both poems handle with a certain playfulness a subject that seems to have no profundity. But in both Miss Moore uses presentation of her subject as a key to open the door to a consideration of ethics.

What kind of armor would help retain wholeness of being? In "His Shield" the recommendation is humility. The poem deals with the defenses of the fabled Presbyter John. This figure, more often called by the shortened title "Prester John," was a legendary, Christian leader vaguely located in Asia or Africa. He was believed to wear a garment of salamander's skin; the poem takes advantage of this detail to make purposeful allusions to the legendary ability of the salamander to survive unscathed in the midst of fires and to the related belief that asbestos was made of salamander skin.

"Everything," the opening stanza comments, "is battle-dressed." An obvious instance of this state is the porcupine; rather elaborate punning and citation allude to the Latin etymology of his name (*porcus,* pig, and *spina,* spine) and to such similar-appearing creatures as the echidna and the European hedgehog who are sometimes mistakenly identified with him. The thorny rhythm of the lines is meant to match their prickly subject matter. But a spiney coat—what because of the etymology of "porcupine" may be called "pig fur"—is not adequate for the speaker of the poem. He will prefer to shield himself in salamander skin; for thus he, like Prester John, will be able to endure the flames of life, indeed, to be a "firebrand," and to avoid drowning: he will be armored against all vicissitudes.

Yet the real shield of Prester John was not physical. His country, characterized by gusto without greed, had gold and rubies enough to make it wealthy, but it remained "unpompous." And Prester John himself, salamander-like, was so shielded against the fires of greed that he styled himself "but presbyter," not pope or bishop. Thus "His shield/was his humility": by refraining from boasting and pomp, he was able to avoid inciting invasion of his realm. Dressed without excess and accompanied only by the retinue customary for a man of moderate tastes, he was nevertheless safer than an armored knight because—like the man in "The Hero"—he had the "power" of remaining not overly concerned about his possessions; he would not let greed or pride force him to give up his freedom in a miserly fear for them.

The lines are yet another of Miss Moore's insistences on the paradox that what she calls "captivity"—the imposition of self-discipline—paradoxically breeds freedom; and they recall also the connection of peace, plenty, and wisdom asserted in "Smooth Gnarled Crape Myrtle." The concluding advice quite logically is that one should find whatever method of cloaking best defends him; but, above all, one should, like Prester John, avoid the pride that tempts the conqueror: "be/dull," not "envied." And one should not equip himself with a "measuring-rod"—make invidious comparisons of his wealth and status with those of others.

The best defense for the individual is humility, a willingness to sacrifice pride; and that this quality may be the best defense for all men in this "sick" world is suggested in " 'Keeping Their

World Large.'" This poem is a counterpart to "In Distrust of Merits," which warned that egocentrism is a major cause of error and war. The soldiers who fight for a "large" world are combatting the smallness of the self narrowed by pride and greed. The poet remarks in "'Keeping Their World Large'" that she would like to see the Italy of arts and crafts, of wisdom and angels, the homeland for various individuals who probably are residents of her own Brooklyn. She would like to see it "this Christmas Day" in "This Christmas Year." We may note that the poem was inspired in part by a quotation printed in the New York *Times* in the summer of 1944 (her notes to the poem say June 7, but the actual date was August 21), and that it appeared in the Autumn, 1944, issue of a magazine. The allusion to Christmas thus is figurative: the time is that of a Christmas, regardless of the calendar, because the poem celebrates a rebirth of what Miss Moore regards as Christian sacrifice and atonement.

Thought of seeing a peaceful, eternal Italy in 1944 brings to mind other paradoxical things the poet would like to find: for example, a silent piano and a "heart that can act against itself." Mention of such a heart brings up in turn the memory of Allied soldiers dying in Italy—dying in a brave willingness to match the sacrifices of Christ and of the apostles; they are willing even to die in vain if, as we can be sure Miss Moore doubts, Christ and his followers died in vain. Against "this way" of winning—victory by sacrifice—all hearts cried out; yet the soldiers, Christlike, continue. Christ and dead soldiers remind the poet of a military cemetery with its rows of white crosses, a vision that "makes us faint"—the poem shifts now to the plural—but that one nevertheless must not turn away from. These soldiers are to be seen as sacrificial offerings for the rest of us; must we, the poem now asks, harm them? Obviously we the living could harm them only by failing to live up to the spirit of their sacrifice. This realization is reinforced by the remark that the soldiers would want only "Tears that don't fall," an inward, spiritual mourning.

The soldiers who represented "Belief in belief," who marched as individuals though in a community of spirit, who in marching to their deaths were "marching to life," acted as Christ did at the crucifixion; they bravely made a sacrifice that their spirit cried out against yet knew was necessary. That silent marching, this spiritual "silence" of the dead soldiers, constitutes a wordless but real message. Their spirits and their bodies, sacrificed to shield us against the "enemy"—both, we may assume, the would-be conqueror and the inward errors of self—were and remain our "shield." Their nobility should inspire us to struggle against the "fat living and self-pity" that are our less physically dangerous but nevertheless threatening enemies. Meanwhile, the poem closes, may the forthright sun shine upon "this sick scene," the whole world where war and error dominate. The poem "Leonardo da Vinci's" shows that Miss Moore uses the sun as a symbol of resurrection. The soldiers' sacrifice represents a rebirth of the Christ spirit, a "Christmas" we should attempt to bring about in our lives.

In Miss Moore's earlier poetry, recommendation of such qualities as restraint and naturalness in behavior was founded on a belief that man is accountable to and is fortified by a world of spirit. Such poems as "'Keeping Their World Large'" demonstrate that in her middle period she had come to take a specifically Christian view of the nature of spirit.

But the high idealism of ultimate sacrifice is not demanded in normal human experience. The last four poems return, therefore, to consideration of choices most of us may expect to be confronted with. "Efforts of Affection" remarks upon the point that love demands nourishment, that it does not come full-blown from some heavenly garden. The opening lines cite various examples of disparity—the Jubal and Jabal of Genesis who, though brothers having similar names, supposedly founded quite different lineages; Shakespeare's mention of hay that has no equal; the astonishing yet commonly experienced stubborn individualism of lovers. After viewing such oppositions, the poem comments "How welcome" it is to see the firm "integration" afforded by "unself-righteousness."

Taking another tack, the poem reflects upon the modest proclamation of a lover that he is not a saint, and it exclaims that his humility shows him to be indeed in the grip of a "sainted obsession." The idea of attraction and of a protesting lover leads to the remark that the bleeding-heart is more attractive than perfume, whereas the elephant's-ear plant does not attempt to disguise what it is. Although both plants have selfish aims, the one is deceptive; the other, forthright. The world affords, in short, examples of disparities and deceptions but also of honesties. These contrasting possibilities may be observed in love; it, like the sun, can heal or can spoil.

Thus man lives in a situation that offers diverse choices.

"Wholeness"—an "integration" including about the same qualities as those found in "wholesomeness"—is best understood not as an absolute but as the result of "efforts of affection." Spiritual unification depends, we deduce, not on attainment of an ideal but upon willingness to strive towards one. Such effort will achieve an integration that is "too tough for infraction." Variations in the style of passages in the poem reinforce the idea of diversity. The first two lines and the next-to-last stanza use a quick tempo and a diction of common words to give information and to make secondary assertions. The second and the last stanzas employ a Latinate diction, slowing the pace to convey their somewhat sententious content. One result is an alternation of playful and serious tones to suggest that the speaker is thoughtful and reasonable, that she has a restraint in assertion because of an ironic realization that wisdom on the nature of "Wholeness" is not yet attained.

Love requires, of course, a certain aggression, an attachment of the self to someone else. That the self should be proffered only with restraint is asserted in "Voracities and Verities Sometimes Are Interacting." The poet remarks that she doesn't like diamonds, preferring the "unobtrusiveness" of emeralds. Even gratitude can at times be annoyingly intrusive. Her preference is for the unflamboyant, the Prester John of "His Shield." Thus poets, for example, should not be immodestly aggressive in their praises and declarations; other creatures, after all, have accomplishments—the elephant can express himself, the tiger can furnish interesting subject matter. Glowing diamonds and assertive poets both obtrude; both are in a sense voracious for attention, making excessive claims on one's senses. Yet, as the title indicates, there is one area in which voracity can lead to truth. One may, the ending declares, be "pardoned" for "love undying." (The phrasing is from the sixth chapter of Ephesians, Revised Standard version.) The lover is necessarily going to violate the tenets of restraint. But he may be forgiven, for in his aggression he will come to a more profound comprehension, to a greater verity than restraint could provide.

There is an unusual crypticism in both "Efforts of Affection" and "Voracities and Verities . . . ," a suddenness of movement and a lack of explanations comparable to the procedures in "Marriage," Miss Moore's early, long consideration of the need for effort and the nature of aggressions in relationships of love. In "Marriage" this abruptness in expression was sometimes confusing. In the two more recent poems the reader must make equal leaps of imagination, but he will find that the poems provide sufficient base for him to take off from. Their quickness and brevity, indeed, seem suited to the intricacy of their content.

Reconciliation of perhaps conflicting desires for integration, love, and unobtrusiveness is a function of the quality that is the subject of "Propriety." In it the poet considers the appropriateness of Brahms's technique, represented as the imitating of such natural sounds as bird songs and of such natural actions as the spiralling of a bird up a tree. These, having "strength at the source," produce "reticence with rigour," the strong and disciplined humility Miss Moore admires. But propriety requires an equal amount of the artfulness "in a minor key" that the poet finds in the work of Bach, the "cheerful firmness" that may be compared with such natural phenomena as the shape of a fir tree. Propriety thus is a harmony of both owl and cat, of wisdom and serenity. It is "not a graceful sadness," a sentimental melancholy; it has "wits" and it resists with humility. The qualities typified by the work of neither Bach nor Brahms should dominate, for the comprehensions of both men are involved in propriety. And both represent a natural fastidiousness "uncursed by self-inspection," a free response to inspiration. Because of its playful tone, its delight in elements of nature, and its suitably cheerful pace, this poem exemplifies the quality it describes.

Collected Poems ends with "Armour's Undermining Modesty," stanzas appropriately presenting Miss Moore's conclusions on the theme of strength through virtue that has been prominent throughout her work. Recollection of a moth that had lit on the poet's wrist—reported in the offhand but artful manner of Robert Frost—brings to mind the intricacy and beauty of the manner in which its wings were "furred." Thought of this delicate, natural accuracy calls up by contrast the blunders of man as he invented the "mis-set" alphabet. From this it is an easy step to humorous mention of the punning motto of a business firm and to a remark upon the prevalence of "faulty etymology."

Since man is unable to deal with the precise even in his mechanical activities, it is no wonder that he and his fellows can announce that "we hate poetry" and the imagery it uses. What man cannot grasp is the indirection by which poetry pursues its goals. If poetry must be explicit, the poet remarks, let us have instead of it "diatribes" and, in place of its harps and

new moons, such direct appeals to the senses as the smell of
iodine and of the acorn from a cork oak. Another alternative
to being tastelessly explicit might be adoption of the imperson-
ality of a deer pictured on a sales poster.

People reject poetry because they mistakenly think it to
be less precise than the matter-of-fact. What is really accurate,
"more precise than precision," however, is "illusion." Thus the
knights of old, such men as the storied seekers of the Holy Grail,
were garbed simply and unobtrusively in the "old Roman
fashion" and not like the ornate knight of modern tale-tellers
who is dressed to play a role rather than appear in natural
simplicity. The knights of the Grail story, dedicated as they
were to virtue, wearing no "armour gilded/or inlaid," did not
let anything, not even the "self," prevent them from being of use
to others. One must not, we gather, let his pride in or protective-
ness toward himself, his armoring of self, prevent him from
communing with others. The armor with which we are to gird
ourselves is to be a spiritual one, a necessary protection from the
arrows of life but not a barrier to brotherhood.

Though Mars—here perhaps in his attributes as god of iron
and of fortitude—can be too zealously protective of the self,
heroes do not need to shun all self-protectiveness. What they
would avoid is obvious enough without their having to write an
"ordinall," an exact list of every sin and folly. Thus the poet
would like to "have a talk with" a hero, to learn from him something of what "excess" is, and also something of the nature of
that spiritual armor that enables him to overcome barriers to
virtue by "undermining" them. This armoring is a product of
humility; unlike gaudy outward armorings, it is not a guise of
innocence covering an inner "depravity" in taste and ethics.

One vested in a mirror-bright but modest spiritual armor
should be able to live up to the vows of a Grail knight and to
practice a deliberate, not merely fortuitous "continence," a term
meaning avoidance of error in ethics. This ability to avoid wrong
is so real that it may be found "objectified"; it exists, so to speak,
in an "innocence" that is true, possessing the "altitude" given by
virtue and an independence that is not hackneyed by self-
gratulation or other immodesties. On the one hand, the poem
concludes, is a "there" occupied by immodesty, by failures in
"continence"; on the other is a "there" offering to the possessor
of true humility that spiritual independence all wish to attain.
Man is the creature who must make choices, "The Pangolin"

said. In "Armour's Undermining Modesty" we are told that the principal alternatives for man are pride or humility. The man of goodwill, the hero, will choose to steel himself in uninsistent virtue.

IV   *Omitted: Seven Discards*

In the period between publication of *Selected Poems* (1935) and *Collected Poems* (1951) Miss Moore published in periodicals seven poems that she did not print in 1951 and has not included in her later books. (An eighth poem, "The Student," is a revision of an earlier poem and is discussed in connection with "The Hero"). Since she has not reprinted them, we may assume that Miss Moore does not wish them to be considered representative. Four of them appeared in the middle and late 1930's. These include "Half Deity" (1935), a long poem on insects that has many fine passages; "Pigeons" (1935), a somewhat playful treatment of the homing pigeon; "See in the Midst of Fair Leaves" (1936), a contrast between the swan and angel, which represent beauty, and man who in his selfishness is often an "arrow turned inward"; and "Walking-Sticks and Paper-Weights and Water Marks" (1936), a long but unified poem using a description of a walk in the country to comment on decorum and craftsmanship. All four need minor revisions to make their intentions or their syntax clear; with such revision, all four would be worth preserving.

The other three poems appeared in the early 1950's. One of these, "We Call Them the Brave" (1951), a treatment of courage, has been mentioned in connection with "In Distrust of Merits." "Pretiolae" (1950), a six-line poem of forty-one words, remains cryptic despite the approximately eighty words in its accompanying notes. "Quoting an Also Private Thought" (1950) is a consideration of similarities in people's thinking and of the resulting temptation to intrude upon one another.

CHAPTER 4

Moralist of Affairs:
Translations and Prose

THE PROGRESSION from the admonitions of Miss Moore's early work to the exposition of need for redemption in the poems of her middle period completes an act of moral commentary. By the mid-1940's she might have had nothing left to write but reiteration. Approaching sixty, she might have become the good grey lady poet, the intelligent eccentric of the coated-paper magazines. But a Marianne Moore would find a way out of such a trap. The way that actually opened for her was translation of the *Fables* of Jean de La Fontaine, a task that enabled her to express a sophisticated, secular but not amoral vision and one that she turned into a triumph. Though her primary creative accomplishment is in her own poetry, translation has been an important area of endeavor for her. A thorough consideration of her writing should include, moreover, her individualistic prose.

I *The* Fables *and Other Translations*

Of course her adult and poetic translation of La Fontaine's *Fables* is not "the same as" his original: it is not the word-for-word Englishing demanded of a college student. Poetry is made up not of words but of a complex of associations and rhythms; Miss Moore's translation is, therefore, not an exercise in lexicography but a venture of thoughtful imagination.

Translation of the complete work was also hard labor. Miss Moore began the task in 1945, after W. H. Auden had suggested her name in response to a publisher's request for a translator. The translation amounts to over three hundred pages; allowing for differences in type and in page size, this is perhaps two and a half times as much verse as she has in *Collected Poems*. In eight years of intensive labor she did the entire work four times over, in addition to making innumerable revisions of individual pieces. She told me that she worked sometimes into the night, sometimes sitting up in bed in the morning. She told Donald Hall (interview in *A Marianne Moore Reader*) of the discouragement she had to overcome when Macmillan decided not to publish the work after she had given it four years of effort, and of the relief she consequently felt when Viking Press accepted it. Her conscience as a craftsman is not yet satisfied: the entire job should be done over, she told me, because, though she likes the "patterns," she is not pleased with many of the rhymes.

Miss Moore as translator applies principles apparent in her own poetry, but she maintains the form and structure of the original. This "pattern" is subjective, however; the real form and structure to her are determined not by logical sequences of rhetoric but by inward movement to a destination. Thus she wrote in the foreword to *A Marianne Moore Reader* that "The rhythm of a translation as motion . . . should suggest the rhythm of the original." The words, she added, should be "very nearly an equivalent of the author's meaning." The "very nearly" is not an alibi for incompetency but a recognition of limitations inherent in language. To maintain the overall movement of thought, she often adds to or subtracts from the content of a poem. Her aim in these alterations is not to improve La Fontaine's story or statement but to maintain its spirit while achieving reasonable compliance with the urgencies of the fable's motion and while meeting the demands of English syntax and metrics. The working principle is also that of John Ciardi, who in the prefatory note to his translation of Dante's *Purgatorio* remarks that theory concerns the poet-translator "only until he picks up his pen . . . and as soon as he lays it down." That is, as an experienced poet Miss Moore operates subjectively: the translation is good when her poetic perceptions assure her of its rightness.

She did not rely entirely upon her own subjectivity; indeed, she had the courage to solicit suggestions and help from a number of friends and authorities whom she thanks in her foreword. As with her frequent use of quotations in her own verse, this willingness to heed others demonstrates both a catholicity of mind and a practical self-assurance that rejects fussy insistence upon self-protectiveness. The chief of these helpers was Ezra Pound, who during much of the eight years Miss Moore was at work on the *Fables* was an inmate of St. Elizabeth's Hospital in Washington, D.C. Miss Moore had of course corresponded with Pound in the heyday of the "new" poetry; she had met him when he was in New York in 1939. Now she made several trips to Washington to confer with him on her translations. She wrote in the foreword that his practice was for her "a governing principle," that she "deduced" from his works the principles of following the "natural order of words," use of active voice, avoidance of "dead words," and use of "rhymes synonymous with gusto." According to Charles Norman's biography *Ezra Pound* (1960), Pound wrote to her after seeing some of the fables in manuscript that she should rid her work of French syntax. He also suggested that she write out the sense in English prose and then versify from that paraphrase —so much heed the working poet pays to the ineffabilities of quasi-romantics who "love" poetry and critics who have never written it!

Miss Moore says that it was La Fontaine's craftsmanship that first drew her to him; she told me, in a somewhat cryptic note, that her work as translator was "educative" to her "ear." But she also says that the task increased her sense of "diplomacy," and in discussing his craftsmanship (foreword to *A Marianne Moore Reader*) she moves easily into citation of "certain lessons." Though craftsmanship was on her mind—a translator, after all, is a performing artist, not primarily a composer—she could not help being aware of the content and must have been pleased by its sophistication.[1]

She must also have been pleased by its quality of presentation, a virtue she noted and re-emphasized in translating the prefatory poem to the Dauphin: for La Fontaine's explanation that the happenings and fiction of his fables "contain truths that serve as lessons," she wrote that they have "Insight confirmed by direct observation." She must have been equally pleased by the fables' freedom from the arbitrary *do's* and *don't's* of "Puritan" tradition, the prohibitions and admonitions that have taught generations of school children to value a trinity of time, money, and work; to believe that virtue always triumphs and evil is always punished; and to accept the fantasies of a Horatio Alger (whose successes typically come, be it noted, not by observation of the moralities preached in the stories but by sheer luck). It is this arbitrary, niggling version of morality that has in the twentieth century condemned the whole notion of moralizing. Our school readers praise the hardworking ant and sneer at the fiddling grasshopper. Yet what is "moral" about letting the grasshopper starve?

La Fontaine's fable of these creatures is intended not to approve or disapprove of the world but to present it as it is. La Fontaine himself in his preface defends the fable as a device for instructing children; in this introduction he cites "The Fox and the Goat" as an example of the fable's capabilities for teaching by means of a tale whose characters appeal to a child's imagination. The story is that of a goat and a fox who, while companionably strolling, grow thirsty and leap into a well to get a drink. They then realize they have no way to get out. The crafty fox suggests that he stand on the goat's horns, a platform from which he can leap to the top. The foolish goat praises the fox's wisdom and enables his escape—only to realize that there is no way out for himself. The fox triumphantly chides him, and goes away.

This is not the kind of tale favored by sentimentalists: it expresses no pity for the goat, who has been left to starve; it allots no punishment to the fox, who has cold-heartedly deserted his companion; and it promises neither the Marines, the Seventh Cavalry, nor Kind Little Boy to effect a last-minute rescue. La Fontaine does not think that grasshoppers who fiddle and goats who err ought to starve, but he recognizes that in this world such is often their fate. Like Miss Moore's own world, La Fontaine's is one wherein peril is always lurking and wisdom calls for courageous forethought.

His emphasis is not on praise or blame; the typical fable is not a story of a contest between virtue and vice, but a contrast of proper and foolish responses to a situation. In "The Eagle, the Sow, and the Cat," for example, a cat's malicious gossip of imaginary dangers so troubles its neighbors that, in misguided attempts to protect their broods, they allow them to starve. The verse editorial of the fable's short final stanza stays with the point that the circumstances have demonstrated: false tongues can do harm. It does not bring in a punishment of the cat or otherwise expand the point beyond the limits of the event itself. We are to see one lesson, the foolishness of the eagle and the sow in failing to detect the meanness of the cat. This does not glorify wrong-doing; but neither does it make martyrs of the stupid. The lesson is that this is a world where wickedness is to be met with; instead of crying over this fact of experience, we should learn to cope with it.

La Fontaine subjects innocence itself to much examination. In "The Wolf and the Lamb," the moral that "Force has the best of any argument" is proved by the tale of a ravenous wolf that, seeking to put a good face on his intentions, turns aside each plea of the guiltless lamb and by a fine process of rationalization justifies himself in eating it. Not only is the lamb consumed despite the rightness of his protests; he is also made to appear somewhat silly because he continues them—he might as well complain of the thunderstorm. The lesson that innocence is not a sufficient armoring against force is surely upheld by a look at the world around us.

Sometimes La Fontaine exhibits his own moral standards by giving contrasting treatments to two fables similar in content. "The Dairymaid and Her Milk-pot" pictures a girl who allows dreams of grand enterprises developing from the sale of her milk to cause her to skip for joy; in so doing she lets her milk container break. La Fontaine comments wryly that we all daydream, that even he had his fantasies of being a king until reality returned to show him that, though he had a king's troubles, he did not have a king's rewards. The tale immediately following this one, "The Cure and the Corpse," has essentially the same point. But the circumstances in it are distasteful: the priest is a mercenary dolt who counts his probable takings from a rich parishioner even while participating in his funeral service. La Fontaine therefore gives him a deserved punishment: death strikes when the coffin suddenly falls on him. The milkmaid's error was petty because it consisted of mere dreaming; the priest's was serious because it was outright greed.

La Fontaine's harsh observations of the workings of the world appear cynical at times. In "The Animals Sick of the Plague," a troop of creatures decides that illness must be punishment for sin, and then determines to sacrifice some particularly sinful member of their company. The lion volunteers himself, but the weaker animals, all seeking favor with him, assure him that he could not be guilty enough to cause their troubles. Similarly they refuse to admit that the tiger, the bear, or any other strong animal could be an important sinner. But when the powerless donkey confesses to the crime of having eaten another's grass, the animals quickly kill him. The point is that judgments depend upon whether one is weak or strong, the weak being likely candidates for condemnation.

Similar practical wisdom appears in "The Vultures and the Pigeons," a story of peacemaking small birds who, in order to halt a senseless war, get big birds to agree among themselves; but the little ones are then ruined because the big birds turn on them. Common sense, that is, bids us to be alert to our own interests because action on principle may be turned against us. Another important moral is that those near the centers of power must be cautious. "The Lion Holds Audience" tells how the king lion banishes both the critical bear and the fawning monkey, letting only the reticent fox escape unpunished. The less perceptive moralist assumes that the way to get ahead in court is to flatter; but La Fontaine shows the bitter truth that the powerful are quite likely to be arbitrary in use of their strength, that the flatterer does not necessarily succeed with them, and that the best armor therefore is circumspection. In these fables La Fontaine is not a cynic attacking ideals of justice and peace-making, nor even formulas for success. He is a realist pointing out that the ideal is by no means always achieved, that the outcome of events is not always controllable. He implies always a contrast between what is and what ought to be, but he does not write in a reforming zeal because he is sophisticated enough to assume that reform is not to be expected within his lifetime. His intent is to alert us to the ways of the world and thus instruct us in the wisdom necessary to cope with it.

Most of the fables exhort to avoidance of error, but occasionally La Fontaine suggests what an ideal life might include. Its essential characteristic would be the humility that leads to contentment with one's situation. Ambition and greed are synonymous. Thus the country mouse finds the city mouse's life too dangerous; the male in "The Two Doves" discovers that he should be content with his wife rather than roam the world for happiness; the mogul in "The Mogul's Dream" learns that the life leading to bliss in the hereafter will be a contemplative one that avoids cares, ambitions, and competition. Such expressions were common in Greek and Roman writing and again in La Fontaine's own late renaissance era; in "The Mogul's Dream" he is paraphrasing passages from Virgil, and his assertion may be to some extent conventional.

But in the fables there are enough passages making use of mirror imagery and valuing withdrawal from the world to suggest that La Fontaine was serious in advocating contemplative solitude. His fullest statement on this point is in "The Judge, the Hospitaler, and the Hermit." Here three saints try different paths to happiness. Two embrace careers helping others, but suffer from ingratitude and listen then to the advice of the third, the hermit, who is the only one to have achieved happiness. He declares that the Almighty set as the principal aim for man the discovery of himself; this can not be achieved by entering worldly competition. La Fontaine cautions that of course society needs the helpful, and that men are not going to give up ambitions overnight; the wealthy and powerful, however, must recognize that the life they adopt to acquire their possessions will prevent the attainment of self-knowledge.

Retreat from the world is not to be fanatical or merely selfish. "The Rat Retired from the World" tells of a weary rat who, ensconced in a rich cheese, became so devoted to his gross comforts that he refused to contribute even to the defense of his city. Not his retirement but his fanaticism, his selfish concentration on his own satisfaction, is to blame for his coldness. What one should want is shown in "The Wishes," a tale of how men given three wishes find the wealth they first ask for burdensome and the poverty they return to not entirely satisfactory; only the wisdom they finally request proves worth having. A principal responsibility to La Fontaine, as to Miss Moore, is to the self. Neither recommends life as a recluse, but both urge a moderation in desire that will leave one free to engage in the contemplation necessary if he is to know himself. Miss Moore goes a step farther, of course; in her translation the third saint recommends seclusion not only to enable acquisition of self-knowledge, but also to allow for a process of "seeking the source": she would scrutinize the self in order to understand what she is convinced are its spiritual origins.

Perhaps the chief contribution of the translation to Miss Moore's own value system is its exemplification of the morality of the man of action. La Fontaine pictures aspects of life Miss Moore does not deal with and, except for her years in teaching and on *The Dial,* has had little direct experience with. She writes of self-reliant individualists, typically of the jerboa or ostrich or basilisk that survives in a man-dominated world without being part of it; her code of ethics is adequate for these individualists. But through La Fontaine's verse she could obtain vicarious experience in a realm of "affairs," of the behavior of the powerful in politics, business, and high society. La Fontaine gives a mature presentation of the code of conduct necessary, or at least advisable, in the world where the individual self is in competition with the striving selves of other individuals. Miss Moore does not necessarily approve of the conduct he depicts, but neither does he. And his presentation of the world as a scene of peril does not conflict with hers. The chief difference is in attitude toward man's future in the dark environment both see. La Fontaine's sophistication makes him a pessimist, unlikely to believe in the possibility of significant moral reform. But her assurance that a saving spirit exists makes her an optimist; she expects that though now weak man can, with proper armoring, be triumphant.

Both poets write of animals; a comparison of their tactics gives insight into their craftsmanship. "I make use of animals to instruct men," La Fontaine told the Dauphin in his dedicatory verses; in the preface he remarked that fables about animals work not only to extend knowledge of animal behavior but also our understanding of ourselves because "we epitomize both the good and the bad in creatures of restricted understanding." His typical fable is a story telling a lesson, usually incorporating a direct statement of the moral. Animals enact roles that the reader knows only human beings would actually carry out; the whole point of a fable is not the fox-ness or stork-ness or lion-ness of its characters, but their resemblance to men, their representation of human qualities. La Fontaine seldom describes the animal, for what is important is not its appearance and its animal nature but its function in the story. He deliberately relies on stock characters, taking advantage of the fact that his reader will see the wolf as rapacious, the fox as sly, the lamb as innocent.

Miss Moore's use of animals in her own verse is quite different. Her presentation is descriptive rather than narrative, and she wants moral or other "meanings" to come from her handling of her materials rather than from the outcome of a story. Her jerboa is clearly a desert rat, not a man in animal clothing; her pangolins and basilisks and lions are equally themselves. They live and act according to their animal natures and not as men who happen to wear feathers or furs. Wishing to avoid stock reactions, she often chooses to deal with exotic animals. Because she lavishes description upon her creatures, her own poetry has more color and ornament than La Fontaine's; even her translation of his work is somewhat less spare than his original because she tucks in bits of description as, for example, in "The Fox and the Crow" and in "The Frog Who Would Be an Ox." But the fable is hardly so esoteric a form that a skilled artist could not successfully operate within it; Miss Moore as translator accepts La Fontaine's form as well as his substance.

She also attempts to match the skill of his technique in order to reproduce the dry, realistic comment that has won international acceptance of his work as a wise and shrewd presentation of human conduct. She not only often succeeds brilliantly in conveying the spirit of his work; she sometimes improves on him. The ending of "The Faithless Depository"—the story of how a merchant subdues a tricky businessman by out-tricking him—is in La Fontaine's version a musing, functional but not particularly pointed comment, translating literally as:

> When the absurd is outlandish, one does it too much honor
> In wishing to combat its error by reasoning:
> It is briefer to go it one better, without heating up the temper.

Miss Moore writes:

> When speech forsakes sound sense, judiciousness forbears.
> Don't aspire to right wrongs or be splitting hairs:
> Best out-Herod your bore and surmount his ill will.

She has quickened the pace, making the expression terse; and she has introduced the notion of splitting hairs and the idea of Herod. She has not in this instance reproduced La Fontaine's world-weary casualness, but she has given what is, all the same, an apt ending for the story.

Often her terse style suitably matches La Fontaine's spareness, and she succeeds at the same time in finding poetic—not merely literal—equivalents for the spirit of his story. A literal translation of the ending of "The Two Doves" is:

> Ah! if my heart dared again to be inflamed!
> Wouldn't I feel more the charm that has given me pause?
>   Have I passed the age for love?

Miss Moore's version reads:

> Ah! might my heart take fire once more in the old way.
> Alert even now to love's spark and, elate,
>   Beat fast as in a former day.

La Fontaine introduces by means of "dared" and the questioning last line a pathos that is reproduced in Miss Moore's translation by the sentimental "old way."

She often reproduces the syllable count and the rhyme scheme of La Fontaine's version. Sometimes she matches his use of other devices as well. Thus in "The Grasshopper and the Ant" she could not duplicate exactly the various repetitions of sound that he employed in the opening lines; but, she told me, she is pleased with the fact that she was able to make use of other sound repetitions suggestive of these (chose . . . chirr; chew . . . chirred . . . chant).

One of the slippery difficulties a translator faces is illustrated by Miss Moore's experience with the concluding lines of this fable. In the complete *Fables* she had her last three lines read:

Night and day, an't you please."
—"Sang, you say? You have put me at ease.
A singer! Excellent. Now dance."

But she discovered that her audience was taking "an't" to be a pun on "ant." She consequently changed the lines; in *A Marianne Moore Reader* they are:

Night and day. Please do not be repelled."
—"Sang? A delight when someone has excelled.
A singer! Excellent. Now dance."

We may note also that this ending, with its comment that singing delights when excellent, is less literal than the earlier version; its effect is to imply that the grasshopper has not excelled, thus making her somewhat more deserving of the harsh rejection she is meeting.

Miss Moore's skill at its best is to be seen in "The Judge, the Hospitaler, and the Hermit." In this fable La Fontaine uses within the last six lines of the long first stanza the rhymes *opposer-reposer,* and *solitaire-salutaire.* She matches this with *ambition-commotion, source-course.* Her first line for the second stanza, "Don't infer that I mean that work is a curse," makes an imperative of his indirect "It is not that work doesn't have to be endured." As often, she is, in making the expression somewhat more pointed, speaking partly in her own voice; but she is also interpreting the gist of what La Fontaine's artful casualness keeps him from saying directly.

There is no need to give an extended comparison of passages. What comparison reveals is not that one poet is better than the other, but that each is himself. Miss Moore as a translator is faithful but not slavish. One should still read La Fontaine in the French. But he will find Miss Moore's "Englishing" of his work to be good poetry in its own right.

Reviewers, predictably, have differed in their opinions: we have few standards for assessment of translations.[2] Though Miss Moore thinks the entire work needs rewriting, the majority of reviewers have praised it; even some who doubt its worth— John Ciardi, Ramon Guthrie, Stephen Spender—have found good words for aspects of it. Only two reviewers have written out-right attacks. Howard Nemerov, himself a talented poet, in a joint review of the *Fables* and Ciardi's version of Dante's *Inferno*, said neither translation is worth while. Mary M. Colum was perhaps the most thoroughly unfavorable, finding neither Miss Moore's expression nor her content suited to the original. Miss Moore herself, always the practical poet, is pleased with some and dissatisfied with other of her translations. She told Lewis Nichols of the New York *Times* that her favorites are "The Dog Who Dropped Substance for Shadow" and "Bitch and Friend"; and she is unhappy with "Middle Age and Two Possible Wives," "The Two Parrots, the King, and His Son," and "The Kite, the King, and the Hunter."

The *Fables* are Miss Moore's major work as a translator. Aided by Elizabeth Mayer, she had earlier published *Rock Crystal* (1945), a translation of a Christmas story from Adalbert Stifter's *Bunte Steine*. This work is perhaps best described as an exercise in style. It tells of two children who lose their way in the Alps on Christmas Eve but are found in the bright sunrise of morning, the implication being that they have been saved by a vision. Miss Moore's retelling is polished but cold. The children never become interesting as people, and the writing is too Latinate in diction and too intricate in syntax for the general reader.

In 1962 Miss Moore published a lively four-act dramatic version of *The Absentee*, Maria Edgeworth's novel of manners. Miss Edgeworth had originally written the story as a play, but rewrote it as a prose tale when Sheridan turned it down. The original stage version has disappeared; Miss Moore's work, therefore, is a restoration. In a typically economical foreword, Miss Moore defends it against possible accusations that it is obsolete by citing famous authors—Ruskin, Scott, Macaulay—who have praised it and by asserting that there are "counterparts everywhere" to its characters. The questions she suggests the critic might ask indicate her interest in both craftsmanship and lessoning: "Does it hold attention? Does any of it apply?" In 1963 Miss Moore published a "retelling" of three of Charles Perrault's tales, "Puss in Boots," "The Sleeping Beauty," and "Cinderella." As with the *Fables,* she employed early manuscripts and worked with the advice of a number of editors and professors.

II *Prose: Varieties of Style*

Though the total of her reviews and essays would come to some hundreds of pages, Miss Moore has not written a unified work of sizable length in prose. She uses prose for literary comment and reviews and for presentation of a variety of opinions and impressions on other topics. In writing on literary topics, she uses an informal but careful style suited to the impressionistic appreciation that she usually presents. She has made it a principle never to print unfavorable comment about other writers, preferring to keep silent rather than to express dispraise. Her comment is never systematic; her reviews and her discussions of literary theory are best characterized as graceful presentation of observations and impressions, the kind of statement one might expect from a good reader rather than from a professional critic. As in her poetry, she often makes artful use of quotation from works she is reviewing and from comments about the works. The whole will be linked not in logical sequences but by juxtapositions similar to those in her verse.

Her personal essays are more idiosyncratic. Occasionally they even verge on the cryptic. Thus in the foreword to *A Marianne Moore Reader* she begins many of her paragraphs with abrupt one-word headings, and skips from topic to topic both within each paragraph and from one paragraph to the next: she often omits "an," "a," and "the" from the start of a sentence, and she makes quick turns in thought and phrasing. All this forces rereading. Passages in "My Crow, Pluto—A Fantasy" are similar. This style is brilliant and often delightful, if at some points too clever. But it is not in any case very common in her work. More typical personal statement is "Brooklyn from Clinton Hill," in which economy of expression gets the reader efficiently and pleasantly through a variety of impressions, accomplishing this individualistically but unobtrusively.

The idiosyncrasy and gusto she favors in all prose style would weary the reader of a long work. But in the short pieces she writes, it often makes for delightful expression of perceptive comment and fresh feeling.

CHAPTER 5

Reaffirmations: Late Period Poems

THROUGH the 1950's and into the 1960's, Miss Moore has remained an active poet. She has put together much of her magazine verse in the volumes *Like a Bulwark* (1957) and *O to Be a Dragon* (1959). Additional pieces appear in *A Marianne Moore Reader* (1961); others have not as yet been collected.

This verse of Miss Moore's late period may be characterized as a reaffirmation. It continues the insistence of her earlier work upon the values of courage, independence, and art; it asserts the need to recognize spirit and the necessity of redemption. Thus it continues to explore the problems of personal and religious experience that have always concerned her.

These are problems that La Fontaine is not concerned with. She, in turn, does not show in her late verse much concern with his world of affairs. She does now exhibit more faith in her fellow man: "Enough," for example, in its tentative approval of the Virginia settlers' endeavors, contrasts with the opinion of "Virginia Britannia" that these efforts failed. Her work in this period is typically compact and allusive, but this is a development of tendencies discernible in her earlier poems. It also shows, especially in *Like a Bulwark,* a developed ability to use humor for serious statement; yet this too is in line with her past work and can scarcely be attributed to translation of the *Fables.* The important influence of La Fontaine is on neither her style nor her values, but upon her idea of a poet's obligations. By 1950, as "Armour's Undermining Modesty" shows, she had grown away from her early admiration for an armoring that would keep one aloof and inviolate; armoring now was to protect one who would be, if not exactly a public figure, at least a "useful" one. Translation of the *Fables,* already well underway, constituted in itself a sallying forth, a sufficient commentary on affairs. In them the properly armored moralist gave the lessoning that the receptive will heed. Miss Moore views herself as free to continue in her later work the exploration of fundamental values that has always been a mission of her poetry.

I *Like a Bulwark*

The eleven poems published in 1956 under the title *Like a Bulwark* had all previously appeared in magazines; in acknowledging permission to reprint them, Miss Moore remarks that "Tom Fool" and "The Staff of Aesculapius" were "much improved" by magazine editors—an acknowledgment few poets would have the courage to print.

The volume opens with "Bulwarked Against Fate," a title indicating an active stance rather than the passive one suggested by the earlier title "At Rest in the Blast." The "object" dealt with is the poet herself, who is conceived of as one of those armored, self-sufficient creatures of whom Miss Moore is fond. The poem opens in the third person, with abrupt one-word sentences ("Affirmed." "Pent.") in the midst of the first two lines giving an appropriately hard, almost staccato tone to the assertion that the object is disciplined by what gives it value. By the third line, the poem is in the second person, directly addressing its object: "you," it says, "take the blame and are inviolate." The connective is "and," not "yet," for the poet wants to present two direct assertions. This creature—the poet's own spirit—thus is self-sacrificing and innocent. But it is also deservedly proud. Though "tempest-tossed," it is not "abased"; it is made compact by the "blast" that assaults it until it becomes fortified, "a bulwark against fate." It is, indeed, compressed to the density of lead.

The closing lines probably are intended as a pun on this experience, the salutary effects of compression reminding the poet of bullets fired in military salute, and this in turn reminding her of the "bulwark" or fortress of spirit that is, in its way, as worthy of formal honors as a military post. The poem is another celebration of the armored spirit; it might also be read as a comment upon poetic style, an assertion of the virtues of compression. It is an example of the highly compact work that Miss Moore thinks is firmest and has the best chance of surviving. The poem is much revised from the magazine version.

From the thoughts of "Old Glory" that closed "Bulwarked Against Fate" it is an easy move to "Apparition of Splendor," which presents the porcupine as an example of the "bulwark." Here what is praised, however, is the creature's "symmetry" with nature. The poem opens with allusions to an animal seemingly "miraculous" that was pictured by Dürer, allusions hinting at spiritual and esthetic status for the porcupine. The third stanza remarks factually that the porcupine has "never shot a quill"; in thus correcting a persistent folk belief, the poem gains an air of authenticity that is supported by the specific descriptions of the animal's barbs that are intermingled in stanzas four and five with further allusions to fictional and fairy-tale porcupines.

Through the first five stanzas we are presented with the half-literal, half-legendary creature that is somehow in harmony with the forest sorrounding it. Belief in the existence of such harmony seems to suggest that the forest, the world itself, shares some of the spiritual element suggested for the porcupine. The last stanza then hails the porcupine for his steadfastness and peacefulness; the editorializing of the stanza grows directly, detail by detail, from the picture already given. If the animal is in part the "apparition" mentioned in the title, it is one of "splendor" because it is a "resister" to the oppressive and the insistent: it is, indeed, like a bulwark. The porcupine is in at least this sense miraculous; though a "thing," it transcends thingness because of its character.

The paradox that both the white and the dark are associated with truthfulness leads to assertion of the value of truthfulness in "Then the Ermine:", a poem treating its subject with an intense seriousness that is not betrayed by the ironic humor that infuses it. Truthfulness is the opening concern, the title and first line alluding to the idealism of Clitophon, son of Kalander in Sir Philip Sidney's *Arcadia*. The poet tells us that she too has idealism, wanting to be regarded as trustworthy in her assertion that she saw a bat abroad in the daytime. In the bat's insecure but courageous persistence in its aims, it reminded her not of heavy-handed "bravado" but of a duke's motto, "I spurn to change or to take fright." This causes her to reflect that she too does not change and is not "craven"—though she cannot say for sure that it would always be difficult to frighten her. The air of thoughtful reflection, of conversational intimacy with the reader, seems intended to carry him along into the more compressed reflections in the last four stanzas. Thought of the bat's "wavering" flight—like that of a jack-in-the-green, the man concealed in boughs who took part in May Day rites—leads to the possibility of failure.

If she does not achieve her aims, she remarks in the fifth stanza, the physiography of Johann Lavater will have "another admirer." Lavater was a Swiss versifier and pastor whose best known work is a study of physiognomy. Both physiography, the description of nature and natural objects, and physiognomy, the study of human appearances, are of interest to Miss Moore herself; she seems to be remarking that if she fails in her own presentations she will admire all the more intensely the skill Lavater demonstrated. His art, it appears, lay particularly in his ability to make the obscure lucid, a skill "now a novelty," the stanza asserts.

Yet, since "nothing's certain," we should allow others the expression of changeability we may not desire in ourselves. A palisandre settee—one decorated with human, animal, and plant figures—may properly show in one and the same scene a crow "in full dress" and a shepherdess, representatives of utter naturalness and of highly artificial dignity. Such obvious expression is acceptable; however, the "wavering" bat and the poet who fears that she may fail have their potential also. The "foiled explosiveness" they represent prophesies action to come that may give success to their efforts though being, paradoxically, "a concealer." Like the bulwark and the armored animals that Miss Moore admires, concealed possibility has power, here a power of "implosion," of bursting inward like the violets depicted by Dürer. The poem closes with the line "even darker," seemingly an allusion to color symbolism in which the violet stands for love of truth. Such color symbolism also perhaps accounts for description of the crow as "ebony violet," and for mention of a shepherdess (who is possibly from Ionia, a province named for the violet). The title seems to indicate a continuation, taking up the ermine that is also a symbol of truth.

Ideal behavior is not quiescent nor dull, but spirited; this is evident in the next two poems, "Tom Fool at Jamaica" and "The Web One Weaves of Italy." Tom Fool was a race horse, much praised by a New York *Times* sportswriter referred to in Miss Moore's notes. She treats the horse, like the porcupine, as an "apparition of splendor"; but her emphasis in dealing with it is upon the belief that excellence of performance indicates the presence of such underlying moral qualities as persistence in the face of difficulty and resolution to perform to the best of one's ability. Comparing the whale that foiled Jonah's attempt to be infallible with the amusing error of a Spanish schoolboy who showed a man on a mule blocked by a snail, the poem says it is preferable for us to imitate the boy. To feel with ardor, as the boy did—this is "submerged magnificence," and this is the quality of Tom Fool.

This consideration of possibility within the improbable may be owing to Miss Moore's own mixed feelings, for she tells us in her notes that, though attracted to the horse by the sportswriter's description, she was bothered by its connection with gambling. In any case, she moves on with comments on the horse, citing a remark that Tom Fool finds the resolution to make the extra spurt that is the "mark of a champion." A bit of playfulness in alluding to a picture of Tom Fool printed on April Fool's Day serves to keep the presentation from over-whelming seriousness, as does the familiar reference to a race-track announcer as "Signor" rather than "Mr." Capossela (he is mentioned deliberately; for, as the poem remarks, he told an interviewer that he does not bet on horse races). The fourth stanza then is a climax: what a moralist can find to admire, after all, is some of the color and seeming artistry of a race scene; for-getting the purpose for a moment, one can enjoy the colors, rhythms, and harmonies. Half humorously, the poet brings the stanza up short with the remark "well—this is a rhapsody." We gather that extended rhapsodizing would be out of place because the purpose of horseracing cannot be excluded from any complete picture.

Rather than continue with the racing scene, she turns in the stanza to consideration of other kinds of "champions." Fittingly she alludes to noted performers of jazz, another quasi-art where-in style is more important than substance. A couple of quick references to race track sights leads to the ending, "But Tom Fool. . . ." The inconclusiveness suggests that complete descrip-tion of the horse's qualities is impossible. Illustrative of Miss Moore's confidence in her ability to include the humorous, almost ludicrous, without destroying a poem is her reference in the last two lines to the sight of "a monkey/on a greyhound"—an example of racing, to be sure, but hardly one to please a fan. Miss Moore of course is suggesting slyly that what is important is the moral excellence sometimes expressed in racing, not degrees of status among gambling enterprises. The poem's exploration of the relation between moral excellence and superior action is well elucidated by Marie Borroff in *College English* (May, 1956).

That spectacle may be nonintellectual but not necessarily mindless is suggested in "The Web One Weaves of Italy." So much goes on in Italy, the poet remarks, that the visitor hardly knows where to turn. What goes on is a list of tourist activities including a crossbow tournament, peach fairs, and mule shows. But these are regarded here as a "modern mythologica/esopica," a series of activities having, like Aesop's fables themselves, moral implications despite—perhaps even because of—their qualities as "nonchalances of the mind." What happens is "quite different" from the formal education given at a Sorbonne; yet it is "not entirely" unlike intellectual enterprise, for in its Aesop-like suggestiveness it is something "more than . . . spectacle." The poem ends with the assertion that "Because the heart is in it all is well." It is the presence of "the heart," we gather, that enables seemingly trivial activities to share some of the qualities of wisdom or knowledge presumably imparted by a university: the heart and the head, though different, are not entirely separate.

The remaining six poems in the volume are occasional pieces, some commissioned by editors for holiday issues of magazines, others celebrating or inspired by an experience. "The Staff of Aesculapius" appeared first in *What's New,* a publication of the Abbott Laboratories. It celebrates the medical researcher for his persistence, his abandonment of "vague speculation," and his willingness to adopt temporary measures while working diligently for permanent ones. Lines two, three, and four of the fourth stanza incorporate an expression from a prose report ("Selective injury to cancer/cells without injury to/normal ones . . .") at the cost of a slight sag in the rhythm, but they preserve the exactness in both tone and statement of the original with a clarity superior to the somewhat artificially poetic syntax used in the fifth stanza to present substance that is equally factual. Yet this stanza serves its purpose as climax, for in Miss Moore's deliberately offhand way it incorporates the remark that as a result of a new surgical technique "what/was inert becomes living." This technique and the scientific medicine it represents are, so the last stanza's question implies, like the marvelous rod of Aesculapius. The rod with its entwined snake is a symbol of the renewal medicine gives to man. The poem, by exploring exact details of medical activity, has found an exemplification of the persistence Miss Moore values.

Chance sight of an impressive tree probably gave rise to "The Sycamore," a poem remarking that there is "grace" in the small as well as in the large. The sycamore, apparently seen in late autumn, appeared an "albino giraffe" that might arouse the envy of either the varicolored or the pure white. The creatures mentioned as perhaps being stirred to envy are much smaller than a tree, and the contrast of their smallness with its grandeur brings on the observation that "there's more than just one kind of grace." There is, for instance, the grace of such small things as flowers and that of the miniature paintings produced by camel-hair brushes. Worthy of preservation by a noted miniaturist, the poem concludes, was "a little dry/thing from the grass"—probably an insect—seen in a field near the great tree; it seemed to feel humble as a mouse before a palace. Seeing grace in both the large and the little, Miss Moore seems in this poem to honor the small and humble.

Another of several Christmas poems by Miss Moore is "Rosemary," which honors Christ's birth by exploring legendary symbolisms of the rosemary plant. Beauty and her son—Venus and Love, "to speak plainly," we are told—braid a festive garland of rosemary at Christmas. The poem in its first two lines makes a point of not at first alluding to Greek mythology, for its theme is Christian. Emphasis on the distinction is suitable, for it prepares the reader for the etymological comment that the plant was "not always rosemary." The English name comes from the Latin *Ros marinus*, "dew of the sea"; in classic times rosemary was associated with Venus as a fellow child of the ocean, and thus with Venus' son Love. *Ros marinus* at first was Anglicized to rosemarine, and was altered to its present form under the influence of the words "rose" and "Mary."

This etymology, and the facts that the Virgin Mary is often referred to by such terms as Star of the Sea and is frequently symbolized by a rose, all have significance in this Christmas poem. Before the plant's association with the Holy Family, it was something other than "rosemary," the poem suggests; the stanza reports the Spanish legend, explained in the notes, that the rosemary originally had a white flower but, as the herb of memory, has remained blue since Mary spread her robe on a clump of it during the flight into Egypt. Yet, the poem cautions, we are to remember this is an actual flower, "not too legendary" to be real in its "pungency." The poem closes with a final remark on the storied and real attributes of the rosemary, both helping to make it "in reality/a kind of Christmas-tree." The plant's "reality," like that of the porcupine in "Apparition of Splendor," is not that of the realist who values only appearances: it is rather a combination of the spiritual and the sensory.

If the whole of reality includes both the natural and an extra-natural, it follows that a means of expressing this must itself succeed in yoking the physical and the spiritual, perhaps in expressing the one through the other. This idea is advanced in "Style," a poem that seems a commentary not only on art but upon all behavior. In choosing presentation of and commentary on Spanish and Basque performers as a device for expressing this idea, Miss Moore seems to be implying need for passion within discipline.

The poem opens with the assertion that style "revives"—apparently it is all too frequently somnolent—in the dancing of Vicente Escudero, whose control and precision extend even to placement of his hat. We in the United States have our own careful performer in Dick Button, the skating champion; but to suggest that we are related to the performers of south-western Europe, Miss Moore also remarks on Etchebaster, the Basque athlete who won an American tennis championship. Mention of Etchebaster prompts remarks upon Soledad, the Spanish woman dancer who performed in the United States in 1950 and 1951. A pun on her name— "aloneness"—reinforces the declaration that Soledad's black garb does not indicate sadness; a series of similes then indicates half a dozen ways one might attempt to describe the precise figures she performed. So admirable, indeed, are her competencies that she may be forgiven her former career as a bullfighter—a concession one realizes Miss Moore would not easily make. The fourth stanza quickly cites an individual characteristic or two for Etchebaster, Vicente Escudero, and Rosario Escudero. Each of these men has his own mode of behavior or favorite hallmark; in each case it is an inseparable part of his style, of the fitting way of expression he has found for himself.

Having explored the possibilities of a variety of comparisons that might enable one to explain the essence of style, the poet now pretends to surrender: the effort ends in defeat, for "There is no suitable simile." At least, however, we gather that style, a manner of expression that is perfectly suited to substance, will join two or more apparently distinct entities. Fitting expression, the poem concludes, is like a conjoinment of the "arcs of seeds" in a banana by a musician; or it may be said to be like a painter's depiction of the face of a musician. The poem ends, fittingly, not with a bit of syllogistic logic but with an exclamatory repetition of the names of the four performers who are its principal characters. This exclamation seems to imply that better than attempting to describe the indescribable is a simple citation of examples.

The paradox that a large-scale opera could appear on an ordinary television screen is explored with some of Miss Moore's humor but with her usual seriousness of purpose in "Logic and 'The Magic Flute,'" written after seeing a color telecast in 1956 of the opera named in the title. Several remarks and puns refer to seashells, which are sometimes associated with Venus, the goddess of love who was born from the ocean; allusions are also made to the wentletrap, an elegant shell once much valued by collectors because of its spiral shape. This shape bears some resemblance to a spiral staircase, a fact indicated in the etymology of its name, and one important enough to cause Miss Moore to include an illustration of the shell in her notes to the poem.

The opera, we are told, seems to carry her "Up winding stair" as though she were lost in a strange theater. The action appeared on a small screen near a magazine rack in the "abalonean gloom" of a darkened living room, and it was accompanied by the "intrusive hum" of the television set's workings; these impressions seemed to fill the room. But the scene then carried the viewers abruptly out of doors, where it seemed that "a demon" roared the question whether one might ever find love. That the "demon" cried "down" stairs of marble perhaps indicates that he had pressed on ahead in a search that also engaged the speaker of the poem; that the stairs were marble suggests an appropriate coldness, and perhaps also is an indirect allusion to the seashell motif. At any rate, we are told, the answer to the query is "simple." We need only "Banish sloth," the tyrant that pretends to fetter us, to keep us from active recognition and acceptance of the "Trapper Love" that, itself a "magic sleuth," will surely find us if we are open to its discovery. "Illogically" but surely, love has by means of the music "woven" the realization that "logic can't unweave," the understanding that to have love we need not compete, need not fight.

From love the concern moves to beatitude in "Blessed Is the Man," a poem of interest not only for its presentation of certain of Miss Moore's own principles but also for its differences from the ideas and techniques of the Beat movement then (1956) in vogue. True beatitude, Miss Moore holds, comes from practice of traditional but far from universally honored values; one arrives at it not by defiance nor by a process of becoming a martyr within his society, but by holding himself aloof. The opening stanza puts together a biblical allusion, a phrase from an attack on President Eisenhower, and a book reviewer's quotation from Lincoln to declare that the man is blessed who does not criticize, who is not given to intemperance and alibis, and who stands firmly for what he thinks is right.

The second stanza alludes to a self-portrait by Giorgione; the fact that his work is usually unsigned serves to caution the reader that the blessed man, though firm in principle, is not a victim of "egomania." Diversity with tolerance makes a "fort," a bulwark that will "armor" the blessed man as he makes decisions on the basis of aptness to a situation, to a principle, and to public interest. This man, a Ulysses in leadership, will find that his fellows of this age "are now political"—as in the La Fontaine tale quoted in stanzas four and five, they have become brutes. Examples are "Brazen authors" who coat the conscience to resist questions raised by "character." In such circumstances, the true nonconformist is blessed; he is the man who, without being "supercilious," will not give in to demands of the crowd. Blessed, finally, is the man whose faith is not "possessiveness," who does not depend on material or psychological advantages for the self, and who is not limited to the evidence of the senses. He is the man who knows that spiritual victory awaits him. This man, whose eyes are "illumined" by spirit, has seen the light of what Miss Moore regards as religious truth.

The blessed man is the "hero" of her early poems, coveting nothing that he has let go. He is now, however, a man whose behavior is ethical not only in its conformity to traditional standards but also in specifically religious ways. He accepts the faith expressed in the Bible (Hebrews 11:3) that "the worlds were framed by the word of God, so that things which are seen were not made of things which do appear." As it differs with the principles of the Beats, so the poem differs with current fashions in literary criticism. Indeed, Miss Moore says in her lecture "Idiosyncrasy" that the poem was written to combat the "denigration," the smart cynicism that she detects whenever a critic comments upon the presence in a piece of writing of the "gusto" that she, for one, thinks vital to literary art.

II   O to Be a Dragon

The fifteen poems brought together in 1959 under the title *O to Be a Dragon* continue the themes of the previous volume. The title poem expresses the wish to have, like the dragon of Chinese legendry, the "power of Heaven"—the ability to infuse the world with moral and spiritual strength without having to give up one's own being. The opening lines allude to Solomon as one who had his wish and remind us that what he desired was "an understanding heart." Miss Moore's own wish typically is for the ability to adopt such guises as may be necessary for defense of the self and for expression of it.

The remaining fourteen poems discover one or another of her values in such diverse subjects as a chameleon, holidays, and baseball games. Assurance is evident in "I May, I Might, I Must," a short declaration of confidence that first appeared in the Bryn Mawr literary magazine *Tipyn O'Bob* in 1909 under the title "Progress." Miss Moore did not reprint this in any volume before *O to Be a Dragon;* that she could revive it after fifty years proves not that there had been no change in her thinking, but rather that in maturity she could safely express the confidence that from a less securely established writer might seem banal. The air of hesitancy, of one talking to himself, conveys the idea of an expression that is being given only after thoughtful consideration.

Another poem from her early years is "To a Chameleon." In a typography suggestive of the way the chameleon might "twine" himself round a grapevine, the poem first addresses the creature and then declares that even firelight reflected by an emerald as "massy" as that of the Dark King could not "snap the spectrum up for food" as the chameleon has done—could not incorporate the varied colors the chameleon is capable of assuming. The emerald is an appropriate jewel for comparison to the greenery in which the chameleon is imagined to be hiding, and the chameleon himself is another in the series of well-defended creatures Miss Moore has hailed throughout her career. In his symmetry with nature he represents perfection of being.

Yet another defensive guise is saluted in "A Jellyfish," which describes briefly the "fluctuating charm" of the creature and then reports that, when one approaches it, its motion is that of quivering and so one will refrain. The poem is in its first lines a simple report of a circumstance; but "quivers" and "abandon" in the last two lines give it a degree of emotional impact. At no point does Miss Moore allude to the notion of the jellyfish as the weak, "spineless," or cowardly creature popular symbolism makes of it. That she can successfully flaunt so fixed a conception proves the rigor of her skill.

"Values in Use" is a deft satire on those who recommend specific language but fail to employ it themselves. The piece begins with a seemingly offhand, conversational remark that itself illustrates the point by specifying what the poet liked in the setting of a literary colloquium. The second, third, and fourth stanzas quote and paraphrase recommendations of a speaker urging his listeners to live by values in their daily lives and to write concretely of them. The poet's question at the end of the fourth stanza—"Am I still abstruse?"—implies, of course, that the speaker she is reporting on has failed to exercise his own recommendation. The closing two stanzas cite the comment of a student who remarked that he understood two of the "big" words used, and they conclude quickly that "Certainly the means must not defeat the end." This ending is itself an abstraction, a generalization; but the reader should note the skill with which the poet leads up to it and, for that matter, the deliberately trite wording of it. Miss Moore avoids the effect of a tacked on moral by so shaping her poem that the ending grows out of the body of the work not as a logical conclusion nor as a piece of cleverness but as an inevitably just remark in a meditative dialogue.

Few careers are shorter than that of a major league baseball player; and changes in the geographical distribution of teams in the 1950's took the Brooklyn Dodgers to Los Angeles. The reader of "Hometown Piece for Messrs. Alston and Reese" must therefore be a fan of some standing if he is to remember all the names and recall the teams and incidents that the poem incorporates. Yet, topical though it is, the poem is invigorating. The direction that it is to have the tune of a popular song that mentioned a mockingbird and a brass ring sets the tone of lively if faintly ironic humor. In view of the disappearance of the Dodgers from Brooklyn, there now is a heavier irony; the loss of the tradition-laden team for monetary reasons left a taste of brass in the mouths of the community's ardent fans.

But the poem's main import was celebration and exhortation. It appeared in a New York newspaper on October 3, 1956, during the World Series, and it is essentially a gently humorous appeal to the Dodgers to "Come on," expressing the heady local patriotism of the fans and incorporating allusions to games of the 1955 and 1956 series and to various players and associated personages, as well as snatches of quotations from newspaper articles. Use of specific names and reference to particular incidents give the poem its air of reality; it is a celebration by one who, so to speak, was there. After citing a noted pitcher's remark that "Everything's getting better and better," the poem further illustrates hometown zest by referring to a humorous salute a Dodger band had ready for visiting tax collectors. The emotional ups and downs of the hopeful fan are reported in a series of stanzas alluding to actual incidents and occasionally slipping into the first person in order to identify poet and reader with the fan; the rhythms, with abrupt shifts in pace and direction, seem to parallel the quick changes in mood of one who follows a lively game closely. Mentions of the superstition of many sports followers, the competence of favorite players, and the "color" and affection of a baseball man who got the club to give the proceeds from a game to a charity, all help build the tribute to the hometown team.

The last two stanzas become slightly more serious, urging the team to overmaster its reputation as a somewhat ridiculous grouping and citing its resources in manpower, tradition, and public support. The poem finds Miss Moore applying the optimism and enthusiasm that she values to a particular instance, and in turn illustrates the presence of these values in her thinking. If too topical for one not an informed fan, it is spirited fun for such a fan and for the reader who is willing to work carefully through the notes and reread them often enough to become at home with the allusions.

The remark that one player "almost dehorned" the opposition, and the playful direction to the Dodgers to "Take off the goat-horns," properly indicate that the conflict is after all not a very "serious" one. But the spirited tone shows it is fun and not to be disparaged, even if it is not to be treated as of ultimate importance.

A more serious production is "Enough," a poem inspired by observation of the 350th anniversary of the settlement at Jamestown. In honor of the settlers' ships the "Godspeed," "Susan Constant," and "Discovery," three United States Air Force jet planes were given the same names and flown non-stop across the Atlantic to Virginia on May 13, 1957. Miss Moore alludes only briefly to these circumstances, but she explores in detail the difficulties, setbacks, and achievements of the settlers to see whether their accomplishment was, taken in the balance, "enough" to initiate the kind of culture she honors. Carefully naming the ships—partly because she enjoys the quaint moralism of their titles—she remarks on how the confident adventurers found their anticipated paradise "too earthly"—a land then of "pests and pestilence."

Stanza five quickly reminds the reader that the settlers' ideals are nevertheless remembered; the next eight stanzas detail the colonists' difficulties and cite an incident illustrative of relations with Indians: Princess Pocahontas finds that in marriage to a white she surrendered her high status yet found her situation "not too tame." The implication seems to be that a judgment on the relations would find good and bad mixed. Three stanzas then specify some of the flowers representative of the careful beauties of present-day Virginia, a passage reminiscent of "Virginia Britannia." But the scene is again changed; there was no time in early Virginia, we are reminded, for the "French effect," for gardening and rhyming. Remarks upon the paradox that "Marriage, tobacco, and slavery" brought a form of liberty—economic stability and security—conclude, fittingly, that no one knows for sure "what is good." This leads to what is probably an echo of Wallace Stevens, the remark that "A museum of the mind 'presents' "; Miss Moore spells out the application at this point as "one can be stronger than events." Reinforcement of this is provided by mention of the disappointed greed of those settlers who thought yellow dirt to be gold, and of the eventual failure of the settlement itself; could the most idealistic, most trusting have been sure that their work was not in vain?

The conclusion is that what the settlers did was indeed "enough": it was a genuine accomplishment because what material gain was achieved was accompanied by "faith." If "proof" of men's material and ideational expectations for the new country was at the time only "partial," the "present faith" made their settlement nevertheless of significance for us, especially if our faith will "mend" the inadequacies of the heritage the settlers left us. One may note especially the absence of sentimentality: the Jamestown settlers are seen to be greedy enough yet not villainous. The mixture of selfishness and faith that motivated them is acknowledged without debunking or prettifying. As in "The Jerboa," greed is recognized; but humor, specificity, and restraint convey a tolerance enabling the poet to communicate her belief that the moral system indicated by the very names of the ships was wrong insofar as it incorporated greed, but was right insofar as it led to decency of behavior. The poem is indicative of Miss Moore's turn in her later work to a more appreciative view of her fellow man. "Virginia Britannia" exposed the failure of the settlers; but "Enough" suggests the possibility, at least, of moral success.

Faith is also the topic of "Melchior Vulpius," a poem celebrating the composer whose works include an anthem in praise of "conquering faith" in God. The power of such an artist is, we are told, something we must "trust," for it cannot be finally understood though it can be acquired and directed. Such art, at least on the level of ingenuity, is also instanced by construction of automatons with lungs of mouse-skin, here imagined as saying "Hallelujah." We assume that the composer is thought to have received his power of expression from on high; man's abilities to parallel the activities of God—and the enormous difference in respective powers—are indicated by the lines on the automaton: the device is to be respected, yet obviously is far inferior in capacity to the creations of God. Manlike, the composer built from "miniature thunder"; yet, godlike, what he built up were "crescendos antidoting death." If this is a paradox, it is, if not explained, at least celebrated by the declaration that it amounts to "love's signature cementing faith," a love of the artist for the spirit firming the faith of all who hear him.

The restorative power of a work of art is honored in "No Better than 'a withered daffodil,'" originally published in *Art News*. For purposes of the poem, Ben Jonson is imagined as having written in "Slow, Slow, Fresh Fount" that he was in the state indicated by Miss Moore's title. (In Jonson's poem it is "nature's pride" that is said to be a withered daffodil; this pride, however, may be a quality in the speaker of the poem). At any rate, Miss Moore's first stanza quotes the fine lines in which Jonson compares the feeling of his speaker to the dripping of melting snow. We would expect Miss Moore to reject such a feeling, for she does not, at least in verse, give way to expressions of despair. Here she does say "I too," but immediately relates how the sight of a green French brocade revived her spirits. She does not communicate this story in the direct fashion of a sermon writer; instead, she gives comparisons that will make the point to our senses—the brocade reminds her of "some lizard in the shade," then of a miniature picture on ivory showing Sir Philip Sidney. These thoughts give her strength back to her: "I too," she now remarks, seem to be "insouciant" as Sidney and "no daffodil." We are not to assume that being insouciant is Miss Moore's typical or ideal state, but rather that it is an apt contrast to the picture of a drooping, melancholy spirit.

Art in its public function and in its individuality are considered in "In the Public Garden," read at an Arts Festival in Boston in June, 1958 (earlier titles were first "A Festival," then "Boston"). The situation of the poet as participant in a public salute to the arts calls up the reflections. The first stanza introduces duality, speaking of a festival "for all" taking place near the Harvard campus that has "made education individual." This leads to mention of "fine" individuals in the conversation of an "almost scriptural" Boston taxi-driver—one who conforms to the newspaper columnists' portrait of cabmen as sages. The environment's beauties are specified in Miss Moore's usual exact detail: a weathervane, iris, snowdrops. The movement in the passage is backward, from summer to spring and finally winter, an ordering perhaps intended to force the reader's attention upon the details by slightly disrupting his expectation.

After these appreciative mentions of individuals and nature, the theme of gratitude enters in the sixth stanza with a quotation from a hymn heard in King's Chapel. A chapel, we are then told, is like a festival in that it involves an exchange—we deduce the exchange of gratitude for grace in a chapel, of attention or pay for inspiration in a festival; but the poem goes on to cite not such expected reciprocations but rarities, the most "unusual" being "silence." This gift may come, we surmise, in a chapel or in a work of art. At any rate, it is said to be as "unattainable" as freedom, and this leads to yet another statement of Miss Moore's belief that freedom and self-discipline are related. This statement she conveys by quoting President Eisenhower and by citing the determination of inmates of a "trans-shipment camp" to earn passage to freedom by selling medicinal herbs, a strategy they could not succeed in if they allowed themselves to become ill. Man is, as the hymn said, child to God; but he will live up to this role only if he disciplines the self.

"Well?," the poet pretends to interrupt. Some, she says, will talk on and on without saying why they have come. Having just praised "silence" and self-discipline, she feels an obligation to be brief. What she is giving us, she says, is neither a madrigal nor a gradual—it is not to be formal, elaborately artistic, but "grateful." The gratitude is aroused by the experience of seeing the assemblage "wish poetry well." Modestly speaking of herself as lacking the "radiance" Romantic tradition assumed poets to have and as commenting quite unofficially, she says that she can nevertheless be glad that the arts have "a home and swans"— both a welcoming physical environment and an esthetically receptive spirit.

She is "happy," finally, that Art—now capitalized—though admired "in general" on such occasions as the festival, remains "actually personal," the product of the artist. The artist needs, and here retains, it would seem, "freedom" to express himself, a freedom consisting in part of a "silence," an absence of demands from the public. Art has its public function, we gather, but this is not to result in pressures upon the artist; Boston, Harvard, and the arts festival thus are gracefully praised for affording opportunity for a hearing without, we gather, imposing demands. The poem does make use of the conventional formula for an invited artist's address to a crowd, disclaiming any thought that the honor is for oneself and expressing gratitude rather for the honor given the art itself. But the conventional here is carefully explored.

Playful delight in the friendliness, peacefulness, and intelligence of the musk ox in "The Arctic Ox (or Goat)" shows Miss Moore's admiration for these qualities. The poem celebrates the animal of the title by detailing his qualities as set down in the magazine article Miss Moore cites as her source. She follows the article closely, even to such humorous directions as "Bury your nose in one when [he is] wet" (said to one who persists in believing the animal to have a musk-like odor). The article expresses the wish that man make use of the animals to adjust his economy to his environment in areas where conventional agricultural practices are destructive or futile. But Miss Moore omits this wish for social betterment; she prefers to indicate through her celebration of the animal her admiration for the qualities it represents. The ninth stanza calls to mind Miss Moore's poem "Rigorists," which remarked upon the salvation of an Eskimo community by the importation of reindeer. In this poem, reindeer are said to seem "over-serious," a remark suggesting that lightness of tone is appropriate in this poem.

The musk ox embodies many of the qualities that Miss Moore admires and that she believes result from inner spirit. The kind of spiritual inspiration she would like to have is defined in "Saint Nicholas," a poem written for a Christmas edition of the *New Yorker* magazine. The poem approaches its goal playfully, but purposefully; the first stanza suggests that a welcome Christmas gift would be a chameleon, thus establishing at once the attitude of moderation in desire that we expect of a poet who values restraint, "silence," and self-discipline. The description of the animal is based on a *Life* magazine photograph of a chameleon which, being behind the bars of a cage in the sunshine, appeared to be striped. Each detail is accurate, including the tightly coiled tail and the slight doubt as to whether one should count six or seven stripes. Another desirable gift, the poem continues, would be a garment of musk-ox fibre and a fancy shirt. Such wishes are, if hardly routine, at least within reasonable expectation. To reinforce the point that her desires are not extreme, Miss Moore in the third stanza declares that she would not want "a trip to Greenland" or to the moon. Let the moon come here and perhaps enable her to garb herself in moonlight—that would be acceptable.

Thought of the moon introduced a note of greater possibility, and the poem moves on to suggest a "yet more rare" desire. Describing Hans von Marées's painting of St. Hubert, Miss Moore mentions the figure's bowed head and erect form, "tense with restraint." The stance is one she honors. Now she repeats, generalizing slightly, her description of the scene; we are to recall that the St. Hubert of legend was so fond of hunting that he neglected his religious duties until one day he met in the forest a stag who bore in his horns a miraculous crucifix that warned him to reform. Hubert, the story goes, thereafter became a noted churchman. Miss Moore's overt request is quite in line with the imaginative but modest desires she has thus far expressed. But in the last four lines of the poem she suggests deeper desire. She maintains the restraint: she does not tell Saint Nicholas what she would like, only that he "must have divined" what it would be. We may deduce that she, like the latter-day Hubert, would desire a vision of Christ. Miss Moore will not state this overtly; her "silence," her self-discipline are too taut to permit a declaration that might smack of Romantic excess. Yet her understatement is, she knows, fully emotive.

"Saint Nicholas" indicated the love for God that is directly the theme of "For February 14th." The strategy for movement is this work is an address to Saint Valentine, asking him if he would welcome as a gift a poem, a diamond, a plant, or some birds. This, of course, is a witty reversal of the customary Valentine's Day exchange of favors between lovers. The series of suggested gifts ends suddenly with the exclamation that such questioning "is the mark of a pest!" Why, the concluding lines ask, do we think only of "animals," of material benefits, when we have thoughts of religion? Why do we not think instead of the fact that "the ark did not sink"—of the love God expresses towards man?

Religious love would develop a unity between God and man, but unity of a different sort is the theme of the last two poems of this volume. "Combat Cultural" honors the lessoning obtained from the sight of two ballet dancers enacting a scene of combat though dressed as twin brothers. The "moral" they point to, the ending says wryly, is the need to unify the elements of any "objective" that represents wisdom and ethical behavior. The work of art, we deduce, should unite whatever diversities it may contain. As often, the poem leads up to its objective with a seeming indirectness, beginning with references to various scenes of active creatures leaping or flying, moving to Russian dances and then to Arctic Russian sack wrestling in which the combatants are blanketed together. From seemingly casual suggestions of physical action the poem moves first to the generalized unity of action in a dance, then to the enforced unity of a sack dance, and finally to the ballet scene which suggests most directly the "moral" Miss Moore draws.

Unity of all men under Christ is an ideal in "Leonardo da Vinci's," a poem based on the painter's famous picture of St. Jerome and the lion. Jerome, we are reminded, was "versed in language"; most of the poem concerns the nonlinguistic but effective symbolism of the lion. We are given in the second and third stanzas the old tale of how Jerome supposedly dressed the wounded paw of a lion that thereupon remained as his companion, of Jerome's suspicion that the beast had eaten an ass, and of the disgrace that consequently came to the lion until he retrieved the ass from a company of thieves. The result was the forging of a strong bond between Jerome and the lion; it was so strong, indeed, we are told, that they became "twinned" in "lionship." Leaned but taught by his troubles, Jerome used his talents in language to put together the Vulgate Bible.

The lion, too, left his contributions, we are told in the last two stanzas. Miss Moore cites use of him as a sign of the zodiac for early summer and the consequent honoring of him by Egyptians because of his connection with the rise of the Nile. And, the poem remarks, in da Vinci's picture the sun seems to imbue Jerome and the lion; the last stanza appropriately gives the direction "blaze on." We are reminded that the sun shone especially during the zodiacal season of Leo and that in Christian mythology the lion, like the sun, traditionally has been emblematic of the resurrection of Christ. The closing words—directing Haile Selassie, emperor of Ethiopia, to shine on as do picture, saint, and beast—form a typical, seemingly casual ending; but it is typical also in having more relevance than may at first appear, for Haile Selassie is referred to as the Lion of Judah, a title that, because of the lion symbolism, is now sometimes used for Christ. Haile Selassie represents the afflicted people Miss Moore has already spoken of in such poems as "In Distrust of Merits"; he also, perhaps, stands for all those who have "lionship," a desire for Christ. The only reliable bulwark for the self will be acquisition of the powers symbolized by the dragon. Miss Moore believes that these will come with acceptance of Christ.

III *Additional Poems*

Miss Moore has continued active publishing. *A Marianne Moore Reader* (1961) gives a sampling of her essays and reviews, twenty-three pieces from *Collected Poems,* twenty-four of the *Fables,* an interview with Miss Moore conducted by Donald Hall, all of *Like a Bulwark* and *O to Be a Dragon,* and five "other poems." Four of these "other" pieces are recent works not previously collected. One poem, "Sun," first appeared in 1916 (as "Fear Is Hope"); revival of it indicates that Miss Moore still agrees with its point—and suggests caution in attempts to divide her work into neat periods. She has also published in magazines a few poems not yet reprinted in a book.

The recent poems continue her major concerns with salvation for the self and recognition of spirit. These are necessary if one is to perform right action, whether his field be writing or baseball. Salvation takes various guises in the five "Other Poems." How the poet who believes in need for self-discipline and restraint may avoid self-centeredness that would lead him to violate unity of expression is the problem of "Tell Me, Tell Me." Excessive individualism may lead one to "obliterate continuity," to "set/flatness on some cindery pinnacle." Thought of a pinnacle leads to the memory of a diamond rosette that appeared, because of its geometric workmanship, to be the product of a "passion for the particular" suited to a Henry James or to a Beatrix Potter. In such a passion, we discover, lies the "refuge" from egocentricity. We may recall that egocentricity means not only ordinary self-centeredness but also the belief that things exist only in the mind, a belief from which particularism will save one. Faith in existence of a realm of spirit does not for Miss Moore deny existence of a realm of "objects."

Joint allusion to James and to Miss Potter is a playful but not merely antic conjunction. The third stanza quotes from James's autobiography about what he termed the "wholesome" avoidance of excessively "literal" elements in his education. Miss Moore uses his phrases in lines describing the mice of Miss Potter's story of the tailor of Gloucester. The tailor, charged with the duty of cutting a coat for the mayor, despite weariness cut the pieces for a masterpiece (of cerise, we are reminded—a color reminiscent of the diamond rosette). He was unable to complete the work because he fell ill, but the mice he had saved from his cat finished it for him. The tailor thus was "rescued" from poverty and despair, and we recall the cry for refuge that opened the poem as Miss Moore announces in the fourth stanza that she is going "to flee."

She will do this by "engineering strategy"; but ironic reference to such strategy as "the viper's traffic-knot" seems to imply that, like the viper in Aesop's tale who injured himself by his own bite, traffic engineers have only helped knot up the flow of vehicles. What she would flee to are "metaphysical" delights.

The way to this refuge, it appears, lies not only in clinging to particulars of experience; it also lies in that silence Miss Moore admires. Might one tell himself, she asks, to hush up? At first she suggests this request might be in French, and playfully puns on R.S.V.P.; but she then turns serious to remark that courtesy hardly makes sense to one who seriously needs to escape from "verbal ferocity." This latter phrase is an apt summation of the faults she suggested in the first stanza; but she avoids letting it serve as climax by attaching with a semi-colon the remark that she is "perplexed."

The puzzlement, we deduce, is over how to remain free from egocentricity; the proper strategy, she now recognizes, is "deference"—a word she first quotes to show its status as an ideal and then uses without quotation marks to indicate accept-ance of it as a practical tactic. Useful deference, one that defends, requires respect for the particulars of experience and a willing-ness to present one's response to these particulars—a poem—without the "verbal ferocity" aroused by "egocentricity."

Playfully conceding that there may be difficulty in following her shifts of thought, Miss Moore presents the final stanza in the guise of an appended précis. It is in actuality a conclusion grow-ing directly out of the materials. Because she is in a plight somewhat analogous to that of Miss Potter's tailor, the poem in making use of his experience is biographical. The tale of the tailor "ended captivity," she tells us, in "two senses." As an event, it released the tailor from despair; as a story, it by its example "rescued" one reader—the poet herself—from "being driven mad by a scold." The tailor was concerned not so much about his own health as about his commission. Reading of him caused her to focus on her work and thus saved her from herself—from the faults of egocentricity.

Salvation for the artistic is also the theme in "Carnegie Hall: Rescued," a poem exulting in the success of the campaign to save New York's famous concert hall from the wrecking crews. This poem draws on a *New Yorker* magazine account of efforts by Isaac Stern, the renowned violinist, to save the hall; but the material, including some of that in quotation marks, is Miss Moore's own. The poem honors Stern in various ways. Since his name in German means "star," she hails him as "Mr. Star." She also refers to him as Diogenes, the Greek philosopher who supposedly went about with a lantern hunting amongst his fellow citizens for one honest man. She makes the appellation

"Saint Diogenes," the "Saint" of course being an honorific. The second stanza, in remarking that the hall "became (becomes)" a "stronghold" for music, seems to be referring to the fact that that hall had long served that function and now will do so again. Perhaps it also suggests the secondary meaning of "becomes"—the hall, though graceless enough, has by long use come to be almost a shrine, and thus a becoming partner to the artistry it houses. The poem's instruction to stress the "ne" in "Carnegie" is properly playful, and wittily parallels the emphasis on music. Also appropriately informal, as a song of exultant triumph may well be, are allusions to the founder as "Andrew C." and to one of the men who helped save the hall, Frederick W. Richmond, as "Mr. R." Their work, we are told, has staved off the menace of real-estate developers who are left cowering like newborn infants.

Stanzas six and seven comment that those who demolish worth-while architectural "glory" are as wrong as the Venetian who did not obey his city's instructions to garb himself decorously in order to present a proper pattern for children to follow. Mentioning a French writer's statement that in youth he dreamed of glory, the poem asks if we must put references to this quality in the past tense; does not that dream find expression in the "glittering" triumph of the campaign to save Carnegie Hall? That musicians have continued to use the hall demonstrates the need for it. This brings up the thought of the praises that "dog" the performer, introducing once again the idea of Diogenes (who is said to have once remarked sarcastically that his title was "dog"). The poem ends with praise of the "glittering" violinist as one who came to the rescue "as if you'd heard yourself performing"—a remark meant not as an implication that the violinist is egotistic, but as an assertion that Stern devoted his full energies to the campaign as might a man who had strong self-interest.

Spiritual resurrection is the theme of "Sun," the poem first published in 1916. Quoting traditional pessimisms that no one may hide from death, it says that this "truth" is not adequate for "us"—for us of freer faith, presumably. It then turns to address the sun, recalling its function as an emblem of Christ's resurrection and hailing it as a splendor from the Orient, a "fiery topaz" that shone through the hand of one who tried to quench it. It is here to stay, we are told, and the second stanza declares in a vivid figure that "holiday" (derived from "holy day," we recall) and "day of wrath" shall be one because together

> . . . wound in a device
> of Moorish gorgeousness, round glasses spun
> to flame as hemispheres of one
> great hour-glass dwindling to a stem . . .

All time, and all times, that is, will be mystically one under the knowledge of the meaning of resurrection. The poem ends with an appeal to the sun to blaze against disbelief, to conquer the "insurgent" who do not as yet accept belief. Miss Moore's typical poem has wit and intensity presented as thoughtful meditation, often as a carefully worked out progression-by-juxtaposition. But in "Sun" her stance is appropriately lyrical.

The title of "Rescue with Yul Brynner" and the note of explanation that the actor was a special consultant to a United Nations commissioner of refugees direct us to see the poem as yet another exploration of the themes of refuge and rescue. As often, Miss Moore begins indirectly, here with praise of the Budapest Symphony and shamefaced remarks on how as "too slow a grower" she did not recognize the difficulties the orchestra worked under when its members were displaced. In the ninth line the poem jumps abruptly to direct comments upon the number of refugees adrift after World War II, the kindness of Canadians who agreed to accept some who were not in good health, and the virtues of Brynner as a visitor to the refugee camps. Allusions to Brynner's guitar and his cloth cap and to his conversations with refugees come from the pictures and text of his book *Bring Forth the Children* (1960); references to him as regal allude to his starring role in the play *The King and I*.

Though flying from camp to camp like a bird, Brynner, the poem says, was not "feathering himself" but instead was showing sincere concern with the plight of the war victims. Picturing him as "twin" to a dancer in *The King and I* and in the moving picture based on it, and thus an enchanter, the poem moves in the last stanza first to a series of staccato notations of his behavior on his inspection trip, then to a contrast between the reality he dealt with in the refugee camps and the glamor of the palace in the drama, and finally to lines praising his deeds as a Christian by punning on the similarity between his first name and the term Yule for the Christmas season. In his actions, he is now a true king, not just a theatrical one; and he is truly Christian in behavior, not just a man whose name has an accidental similarity to a term for the season of Christ's birth.

The theme of salvation is continued in "To Victor Hugo of My Crow Pluto," a poem telling how the poet enjoyed a pet crow but released it because a crow, even when walking, has the look of one who wears wings. For a prose account of her relationship with the bird, the reader may turn to her essay "My Crow, Pluto—a Fantasy," reprinted in *A Marianne Moore Reader*; the poem and the essay originally appeared on facing pages in *Harper's Bazaar* (October, 1961). The poem is affectionate in tone; it makes use of a short line, includes much alliteration and repetition of such sounds as "tuttuto/vagabondo," and rhymes throughout on "u" and "o" sounds. (In the essay, Miss Moore says that she addressed the bird alternately as Plato or Pluto, depending on the vowel sounds in preceding words.) All this works together to give comic effect. This effect is heightened by use of "esperanto madinusa," much of the last two thirds of the poem being in this idiom that, the essay says, she used in talking to the bird; she furnished with the poem a word list for "those who might not resent" it.

She tells us with mock seriousness for four of the brief stanzas that the crow is a "true Plato" because he meets Victor Hugo's description as a creature that always seems to possess talents superior to those an unimaginative observer of its pigeon-toed walk might see. The poet recognized the bird's ability to speak and, as she remarks in the essay, his competence at petty thievery. These talents presumably made him worth money to her, but she declares that she lives in the belief that profit is a dead weight; she refuses to profit from her avian friend. Thus, though the bird was a jewel to her, she recognized his essential nature as a free spirit and let him go. The poem is another of Miss Moore's expressions of the need to recognize spirit beneath appearances.

Athletics and writing are both to an extent public arts; and each in its own way requires for skilled performance an infusion of spirit. Two recent magazine poems explore these relationships. The nature of beauty is a theme of "Baseball and Writing" (*New Yorker*, December 9, 1961), a poem making typical use of humorous rhymes ("pedagogy"—"prodigy"), abrupt shifts in rhythm, and citation of names of living people to establish a familiar, conversational tone which reinforces the remark of the last stanza that one—whether baseball player or, we deduce, writer—should "bear down" at his work but "Enjoy it." The opening stanza says excitement over writing or baseball is not mere "fanaticism," though it arouses a "fever" in its "victim."

Bantering about the point, Miss Moore mentions the *"Owlman"* (her italics) in the pressbox—a reference to the sportswriters and broadcasters assigned to night games and to their role as public wisemen. Several stanzas praise the skills of various baseball players, most of them New York Yankees. Since we have been warned by the title and by the first stanza to watch for analogies with writing, we are likely to read such a remark as "concentrates promote victory" as significant of Miss Moore's esthetic theory, though as usual the generalization is grounded in the specifics of a seemingly very different area—in this case, a listing of supposed health foods.

The complexity of Miss Moore's attitudes is indicated by her willingness to link baseball with writing; this linking gives a profundity to such lines as "Pitching is a large subject"—a remark conveying a truth in the light of humor. So too the sixth stanza, listing some of the "imponderables"—the hazards the player faces—notes such actual physical dangers as muscle kinks and spike wounds, yet mentions the pains of celebrity with the hardly serious exclamation "Drat it!" and intermixes play on sounds with its remark that "the Stadium is an adastrium." The stadium—the arena, we assume, of both the athlete and the writer—is the home of "stars," a designation not only of celebrities but also of personages whose values are admirable. Thought of stars leads to the appropriate closing salute to Orion, the symbol of that strength and skill which create the beauty Miss Moore finds in expert performance whether in the arena or on the page. The techniques in "Baseball and Writing" are much the same as those in "Hometown Piece for Messrs. Alston and Reese." But Miss Moore was deliberately more topical in the poem written for publication at the height of a World Series fever, and the allusions in it to players now half-forgotten are something of a chore for the reader to master. In "Baseball and Writing," in contrast, the topical allusions, though sufficient to ground the poem in particulars, hardly matter to the "story."

Analogy between the artistic and the athletic also serves in "Blue Bug" (*New Yorker*, May 26, 1962) to suggest the importance of spirit. Explaining that her title is the name of a polo pony she saw pictured in *Sports Illustrated* (November 13, 1961), Miss Moore draws attention to a kinship between herself and the pony: the animal recognizes the recognition in her eye. She won't ask how he got his odd name, she says; she comments on the intrusiveness of those who pester one with questions (an idea she also discussed in "Saint Nicholas"). Then, as if interrupting a conversation, she breaks in abruptly with the declaration that "I've guessed" and goes on to describe the pony as resembling an artist's dragonfly in its ability to make quick turns in direction. This description leads to analogy between the pony's abilities and the intricacies of a Chinese melody. She remarks that the tune gives an accurate "version" of the pony's varied movements in polo.

Having found a similarity between herself and the pony and having also asserted a resemblance between him and works of art, Miss Moore climaxes the analogy by "restating" it. Though "polo" actually comes from the Tibetan word for the ball used in the game, it looks like a Romance language word, a fact she takes advantage of to obtain a bit of wordsmanship implying a similarity between "polo" (she translates this as "I turn"), "*polos*" (plural of a Spanish word for the polar axis of a spinning object), and the name of the game. She, the artist, turns on a "pivot" just as do the pony and the Chinese tune, we are told. The implication is that, diverse as all these may be, there is a kinship because all turn on a pivot of spirit. The poem recognizes that the analogy may be "a little elaborate," but explains, in Miss Moore's usual deftly casual manner, that such a relationship between the idea of revolving and the thought of a "pastime" was suggested by thought of Odilon Redon, a French post-impressionist painter. The painter's name itself must have pleased Miss Moore by its sounds. And she doubtless approves of his assertions that once an artist has mastered his language, he should be free to deal with subjects drawn not only from direct observation but also from history and poetry. As "Baseball and Writing" found that the artist and the athlete should "bear down" but "enjoy it," so in "Blue Bug" it is remarked that the art Redon preferred was a "pastime that is work." One should have the physical control and the alert mentality of a Chinese acrobat; the closing stanza particularizes this. In it, Miss Moore as ever grounds her generalization in a specific picture.

References to a Chinese tune and to a Chinese acrobat have a general appropriateness in that polo came to the West from the Orient; they also remind the reader of the admiration and attention Miss Moore gives Chinese artistry in "Nine Nectarines" and in "O to Be a Dragon." Whether the performer is from China or from Brooklyn, if he is to be bulwarked for right action by means of acquiring the powers of the dragon, he must recognize the spiritual element that gives unity to experiences acrobatic, athletic, or artistic. It unifies seemingly disparate qualities of character also. "Charity Overcoming Envy" (*New Yorker*, March 30, 1963) shows us charity mastering the envy that is yoked to it by convincing it that its self-pity is misguided. This victory shows that it is not necessary to delay hopes for achievement simply because the ethical may be linked to error by a "Gordian knot."

CHAPTER *6*

Accomplishments

I T IS TOO EARLY to make a final assessment of Miss Moore's contribution to the stream of American poetry. But final assessments are hardly required by the reader who is interested in seeing what modifications can be made in his awarenesses by a perceptive, dedicated, and highly talented poet.

I *Literary Reputation*

Miss Moore's work has been an interweaving of perception and creation, the two reinforcing and extending each other: her interest has been in exploring the details of her "object" in order to give both an accurate delineation of it and a suggestive presentation of the values she believes it to exemplify. In so doing, she has pleased nearly all the prominent members of her poetic generation. That such fellow Objectivists as Williams and Stevens would praise her is perhaps to be expected, since she has shared their emphasis on "the thing itself" and has, indeed, refined the tactics of precise presentation rather more than either of them. Perhaps surprising at first glance is the early and continued recognition of her abilities by Ezra Pound and T. S. Eliot, both of whom have worked to perpetuate what they see as a tradition of poetry in English. Miss Moore, after all, has been an independent spirit, hardly a deliberate extender of a tradition. Yet the competencies of both Pound and Eliot are such that one need not be surprised to find them recognizing talents that differ from their own. Miss Moore's care with language draws their admiration, and it probably also accounts for the continued interest in her work of such critics as Yvor Winters, Kenneth Burke, R. P. Blackmur, and Morton Dauwen Zabel. The admiration of most of her significant contemporaries is indicated by their letters and articles (referred to in the bibliography of this book) as well as by such semi-official recognitions as the awards and prizes that have been showered upon her.

Miss Moore has not lived in an ambience of unremitting praise, however. Despite the applause of her major contemporaries, most of her work was out of print when in 1951, at the age of sixty-four, she published *Collected Poems*. It is not surprising that the vast public ignored her, for it ignores all poets save those who happen to appear paternal on the television screen. What is more surprising is the neglect of her work by the academicians who in our society function as intermediaries between public and poet, the teachers and students who read and occasionally buy poetry, and write the books and articles that presumably help spread and sustain interest in it. One aware of the plethora of doctoral dissertations on even sub-literary American writers may be surprised to discover that there has been only one such study devoted to Miss Moore's work. There has been a handful of Master's theses, but these of course are predestined for an academic limbo. The New York Public Library bibliography has twelve pages under the heading "Writings About Marianne Moore," but these include five pages listing book reviews, and many of the pieces under the heading "Periodical Articles" are actually only reviews. Several significant articles are listed in the bibliography to this book; most of the rest of the writing about Miss Moore's work is appreciative comment: it registers approval but seldom comes to grips with the poetry itself.

Praise from her peers and neglect from the academicians and the public make up most of the story of Miss Moore's reputation. But there has been occasional outright dispraise. This has come, as might be expected, from critics and reviewers who cling to what they conceive to be validities of Romantic practice and therefore scorn most "modern" poetry. Early, strong objections came from Margaret Anderson of the *Little Review*, who in 1918 asserted that Miss Moore wrote intellectually whereas real poetry should not be "made from, nor read with, the mind" and that Miss Moore wrote from "the phenomenal world" whereas real poets deal with "the noumenal world."[1] Since Miss Anderson reprinted these remarks in 1953, one assumes that they represent a continuing position.

Another early objector was Louis Untermeyer, anthologist and poet in his own right, who declared flatly in 1923 that

Miss Moore's work had as of that date received little attention because "she is not, in spite of the pattern of her lines, a poet."[2] He said that she did not appreciate rhyme, that her work lacked the "lift" and "ecstasy" of poetry, and that she ought to devote herself to prose because the "critical faculty" dominated her talents. Praises faint, though not necessarily intended to damn, came a couple of decades later from Oscar Cargill, who in 1941 cited examples of fine phrasing from Miss Moore's work but doubted that real poetry could be made from "things" and suspected her of admiring "novelty for its own sake" and even of deliberately seeking praise from reviewers by artfully salting her work with such expressions as "unconscious fastidiousness."[3]

Babette Deutsch, a capable poet herself and one of the best-known historians of American poetry, also gave only carefully qualified praise to Miss Moore's work. In 1935 she wrote that Miss Moore "for emotion . . . substitutes observation, sensation, and reflection," though praising her "discerning eye" and "discriminating vocabulary";[4] in 1952 she was careful to remark that "Such poetry may not rouse us to the most profound response," though she praised Miss Moore's precision and "design."[5] These poets and critics are not, be it noted, the reactionaries of so-called popular art, whose dismissal of all "modern" work is founded on ignorance. Yet, conceding that their objections are based on principle, one may wonder why principles of distinctively Romantic practice are assumed to have eternal validity—or, to put the matter more accurately, whether quasi-Romantic objections do not in truth confuse mere technique with principle: is obvious musicality, for example, a necessary component of all poetry?

II   *Contribution to Tradition*

Neoromantic objections do serve at least one useful purpose: they indicate something of the nature of Miss Moore's contribution to the tradition of poetry in America and, for that matter, to the poetic tradition America shares with Europe. It is exactly in embracing areas of experience rejected by Romantic versifiers that she, with such contemporaries as Williams and Stevens, has greatly broadened the range of concern and of possibility for poetry. As Roy Harvey Pearce points out, she has limited herself more strictly to the "thing" than either Williams or Stevens;[6] moreover, she has dealt with a more limited range of "things" than either of these Objectivists. But the effect has been not a narrowing but a focusing: if she avoids the desperate inclusiveness of Williams and the philosophical questionings of Stevens, she succeeds in getting down an exact presentation of "objects" that are part of the American scene; and she makes use of this realism in subject matter to assert the importance of values she considers to be necessary in American as in all human experience. Her commonsensical approach to her own work and her assumption of a universal validity for good poetry are well indicated in the contrast between the responses she and Williams supplied to a questionnaire asking whether it is "nonsense to talk of a typical American poem."[7] Williams typically gave a long, rambling assertion of the need for discovery and exploitation of a distinctively American "tongue"; Miss Moore remarked simply that she does not see how one can speak of a typically American poem, that Americans achieve poetry not by some species of literary nationalism but by drawing on such universal sources as "depth of experience, imagination, and 'ear.'"

Like Williams, she has followed Whitman's injunctions that the poet should make use of the materials of his own experience. But unlike either Williams or Whitman, she has refused to see a special virtue in the wide-ranging catalog of quickly noted details: she has quietly persisted in the thorough exploration of each object in order to understand not only its presence and appearance but also what she conceives to be its significances. If she continues what Pearce calls the "Adamic" tradition, the reason is not that she honors the barbaric yawp but that she believes the poet should make poetry out of what he experiences. In sticking to her last, she has built well. In refusing to be merely pretty, in determinedly rejecting any temptation to engage in the sentimentalities of standard feminine poetic practice, she has avoided the damning epithet "lady poet": almost alone among American women writers, she is treated as intellectually and esthetically a "poet." Louise Bogan, an admiring contemporary, recognized this fact in observing that Miss Moore understands that the poet should transfer to his reader not sensations but understandings.[8]

It is this achievement of a valid profundity, without fakery of aim or emotion, that caused Lionel Trilling to list her poetry, along with that of Stevens and Cummings, as an example of American creativity that will reward "a mature reader" more substantially than the work of all but a handful of American

writers of prose fiction.[9] It also seems to be what T. S. Eliot
meant when he wrote in his introduction to her *Selected Poems*
that she is "one of those few who have done the language some
service in my lifetime." The old-fashioned way of putting
Eliot's statement is to say that Miss Moore's work wears well,
that it seems likely to outlast flashier, noisier writing of better-
known contemporaries because it performs superbly within the
area of its concern.

III   *An Afterword: Ethics and Esthetics*

Miss Moore in her early work admired an aloof individualism
that would armor the self against assaults of ambition, possessions, and other people. Her hero was the desert jerboa that
in its sparse but natural existence made no demands on others
and asked nothing of them. Courage and naturalness remain
important in her system of values, but in the works of her
middle years she began to consider that man, though sharing
the needs of all living creatures, has obligations and capacities
beyond those of the animal. Man must recognize that there are
questions that appearances cannot answer, that the quiet triumph
possible within his limitations requires of him a willingness to
recognize "as if's" in existence. A proper armoring will steel the
self not for mere withdrawal but for usefulness: the hero is
exemplified by the soldier whose sacrificial death may help
us redeem our sick selves. Miss Moore expanded her commentary
by translating La Fontaine, thus functioning as a moralist of
affairs. In her late period she has reaffirmed the value of
courageous individualism and the need to recognize the unity
of spirit with appearance. Though there are specifically Christian
expressions in her early period, most of her work into the 1930's
is without direct religious content. In her middle and late periods
she becomes specifically though not narrowly Christian, hoping
for a vision and meditating on the need for redemption and
resurrection. The hero is the blessed, unaccommodating man
who follows not fashion but spirit; he is the lion-like, pacific
yet passionate man who achieves a salvation enabling him to
create art.

Her moral commentary is serious and deliberate—not a mere
"subject matter" that may be separated from her art. Yet her
writing is not unduly didactic. She has achieved poetic art
because she has worked as an Objectivist. What she gives is the

experience of the "object" that is the topic of her poem, whether that object is an animal, quotation, or philosophical reflection. She gives not a statement abstracted from the experience, but the "thing itself," the experience in its wholeness. Moral bearings are an inextricable part of this experience, and they take their due place in a presentation of it.

Neither assertion of ethics nor proficiency in technique could make her a poet. The art of her performance lies in the quiet, idiosyncratic "gusto" she brings to presentation. Explication is at most introductory. It omits all the humor and most of the irony, and it can do nothing with the spirited realization that comes with an experience of Miss Moore's poetry. For the reader, the "thing itself" is—should be—the poem.

Notes and References

Chapter One

1. "Religion and the Intellectuals," *Partisan Review*, XVII (February, 1950), 137-38.
2. I am indebted to Sister M. Hilda of Marygrove College and to Professor Arthur Eastman of the University of Michigan for observations upon the meaning of the title.
3. Unless otherwise attributed, quotations and descriptions are from an interview Miss Moore granted me in 1962. Other sources are:

"Best Living Poet," *Newsweek*, 38 (December 24, 1951), 69-71.

Current Biography (New York, 1952), pp. 435–37.

Stanley J. Kunitz and Howard Haycraft (eds.), *Twentieth Century Authors* (New York, 1942); and Stanley J. Kunitz (ed.), "First Supplement" to *Twentieth Century Authors* (New York, 1955).

Marianne Moore, "Brooklyn from Clinton Hill," *A Marianne Moore Reader* (New York, 1961), pp. 182-92.

Marianne Moore, "*The Dial*: a Retrospect," *Predilections* (New York, 1955), pp. 103-14.

Ezra Pound (see Selected Bibliography below).

Winthrop Sergeant, "Humility, Concentration, and Gusto," *New Yorker*, XXXII (February 16, 1957), 38ff.

William Carlos Williams (see Selected Bibliography below).

Chapter Four

1. An enlightening brief study is Odette de Mourgues, *La Fontaine: Fables* (London, 1960).
2. Reviews of the *Fables* translation are listed in the New York Public Library bibliography (see below).

Chapter Six

1. Reprinted in Margaret Anderson (ed.), *The Little Review Anthology* (New York, 1953), pp. 187-88.
2. Louis Untermeyer, *American Poetry Since 1900* (New York, 1923), p. 363.
3. Oscar Cargill, *Intellectual America* (New York, 1941), pp. 299-304.
4. Babette Deutsch, *This Modern Poetry* (New York, 1935), p. 94.

5. Babette Deutsch, *Poetry in Our Time* (New York, 1952), p. 92.

6. Roy Harvey Pearce, *The Continuity of American Poetry* (Princeton, N. J., 1961), p. 374.

7. Balachandra Rajan (ed.), *Modern American Poetry* (New York, 1952), pp. 182-83.

8. Louise Bogan, "Reading Contemporary Poetry," *College English*, XIV (February, 1953), 260.

9. Lionel Trilling, "The Meaning of a Literary Idea," in *The Liberal Imagination* (New York, 1950), p. 294.

Selected Bibliography

PRIMARY SOURCES

This list omits brief publications now incorporated in one or another of the volumes listed; it also omits minor translations.

Poems. London: The Egoist Press, 1921.
Observations. New York: The Dial Press, 1924.
Selected Poems. New York: The Macmillan Co., 1935. Reprints most of *Poems* and adds new pieces.
What Are Years. New York: The Macmillan Co., 1941.
Nevertheless. New York: The Macmillan Co., 1944.
Collected Poems. New York: The Macmillan Co., 1951. Reprints most of the work from previous volumes, often with alterations, and adds new pieces.
The Fables of La Fontaine. New York: The Viking Press, 1954.
Predilections. New York: The Viking Press, 1955. A selection of essays and reviews.
Like a Bulwark. New York: The Viking Press, 1956.
O to Be a Dragon. New York: The Viking Press, 1959.
A Marianne Moore Reader. New York: The Viking Press, 1961. Includes poetry, essays, fables, the Ford letters, and an interview conducted by Donald Hall.
The Absentee. New York: House of Books, 1962. Four-act comedy version of a prose tale by Maria Edgeworth.

SECONDARY SOURCES

There are no books other than this one devoted to Miss Moore. A complete bibliography of essays and articles by and about her, as well as of her poetry, was published in 1958 by the New York Public Library (Eugene P. Sheehy and Kenneth A. Lohf, compilers, *The Achievement of Marianne Moore*). The following listing is, therefore, only a sampling of important comment.

1. Articles

BLACKMUR, R. P. "The Method of Marianne Moore." *The Double Agent.* New York: Arrow Editions, 1935. Reprinted in *Language as Gesture.* New York: Harcourt, Brace and Co., 1952. Relates the esthetic principles she asserts in *Selected Poems* to her own accomplishment, finding her usually highly successful.

BOGAN, LOUISE. "Reading Contemporary Poetry," *College English,* XIV (February, 1953), 255-60. Demonstrates Miss Moore's proficiency at drawing comment from particulars and points to her work as representative of modern achievements.

BORROFF, MARIE. " 'Tom Fool at Jamaica' by Marianne Moore: Meaning and Structure," *College English,* XVII (May, 1956), 466-69. Studies Miss Moore's ability at "tacit embodiment of morally significant qualities in particular beings and actions."

BRUMBAUGH, THOMAS B. "Concerning Marianne Moore's Museum," *Twentieth Century Literature,* I (January, 1956), 191-95. Examines her use of objects of art as topics for poems.

BURKE, KENNETH. "Motives and Motifs in the Poetry of Marianne Moore," *Accent,* II (Spring, 1942), 157-69. Analysis of her Objectivism, examining its relation to her themes and imagery to demonstrate why her work is poetry rather than reporting.

ELIOT, T. S. Introduction to *Selected Poems.* Praises her as one of the few who make a contribution to the language, and as a presenter of "genuineness."

FRANKENBERG, LLOYD. "Marianne Moore's Imaginary Garden." *Pleasure Dome.* Boston: Houghton Mifflin Co., 1949. Points to the "technical virtuosity" of many individual poems to establish that Miss Moore works through realism to arrive at emotion.

JARRELL, RANDALL. *Poetry and the Age.* New York: Alfred A. Knopf, 1953. Contains two appreciative essays, "The Humble Animal" and "Her Shield."

PEARCE, ROY HARVEY. *The Continuity of American Poetry.* Princeton, N. J.: Princeton University Press, 1961. In Chapter 8 deals with Williams, E. E. Cummings, Conrad Aiken, and Miss Moore as representatives of "the Individualist Tradition," finding her not only to have faults of fussiness but also to have virtues of civility and perspective.

POUND, EZRA. There is no important single essay on her work by Pound, but his advice and influence have been valuable. Indications of this are scattered through the correspondence and comment in: D. D. Paige, ed. *The Letters of Ezra Pound 1907-1941.* New York: Harcourt, Brace and Co., 1950; and Charles Norman. *Ezra Pound.* New York: The Macmillan Co., 1960.

SNODGRASS, W. D. "Elegance in Marianne Moore," *Western Review,* XIX (Autumn, 1954), 57-64. Discussion of techniques, including her prosody.

STEVENS, WALLACE. "About One of Marianne Moore's Poems," *The Necessary Angel.* New York: Alfred A. Knopf, 1951.

————. "A Poet that Matters," *Opus Posthumous.* Samuel French Morse, ed. New York: Alfred A. Knopf, 1957. This listing and the one above are short reviews that praise her for achieving "reality" of presentation.

WILLIAMS, WILLIAM CARLOS. Williams has often written appreciatively of Miss Moore as a person and as a poet. Cf. *Selected Essays.* New York: Random House, 1954; *The Autobiography of William Carlos Williams.* New York: Random House, 1951; and John C. Thirlwall, ed. *The Selected Letters of William Carlos Williams.* New York: McDowell, Obolensky, 1957.

WINTERS, YVOR. "Holiday and Day of Wrath," *Poetry,* XXVI (April, 1925), 39-44. Review of *Observations;* praises it by declaring that apparent ambiguities of technique and form are functional. See also Winters' *Primitivism and Decadence.* New York: Arrow Editions, 1937.

ZABEL, MORTON DAUWEN. "A Literalist of the Imagination," *Poetry,* XLVII (March, 1936), 326-36; reprinted in *Literary Opinion in America.* Rev. ed. New York: Harper & Brothers, 1951. Says that seeming "discouragements" of her eccentricity and intellectual irony prove to contribute to her purpose.

2. *Miscellaneous*

MARIANNE MOORE issue, *Quarterly Review of Literature,* IV (1948). Contains a variety of appreciations and articles, including pieces by Williams, Elizabeth Bishop, John Crowe Ransom, Wallace Stevens, Louise Bogan, Vivienne Koch, Wallace Fowlie, Cleanth Brooks, and others.

REES, RALPH. *The Imagery of Marianne Moore,* unpublished Ph.D. dissertation, Pennsylvania State University, 1956. Available as #19, 319, University Microfilms, Ann Arbor, Michigan. A perceptive study of her "armoring," showing how her imagery contributes to it and how, as a result, she is a realist of the imagination. Contains useful incidental discussions of such matters as her techniques, use of animals, and fondness for quotations. Bibliography gives a list of poems in anthologies and a list of books with passages commenting on her work.

Index

Nichols, Lewis, 128
"Nine Nectarines" (also "Nine Nectarines and Other Porcelain"), 27, 55-56, 61, 86, 158
"No Better than 'a Withered Daffodil,'" 145-46
Norman, Charles, 120
"No Swan So Fine," 49-50, 68
"A Note on the Notes," 27, 28
" 'Nothing Will Cure the Sick Lion but to Eat an Ape,'" 77-78, 79
"Not Ideas About the Thing," 60
"Novices," 71-72, 80

Objectivism, 18-19, 159, 161-62, 163-64
An "Objectivists" Anthology, 18
"An Octopus," 28, 74-75, 77, 81
Ogden Memorial Church, 32
100 Modern Poems, 108
"Other Poems," 150-55
Others (anthologies), 33, 84; (magazine), 33
"O to Be a Dragon!," 28, 158

"The Pangolin," 29, 97-100, 103, 116-17
"The Paper Nautilus," 87, 94, 100-1, 102, 106
Papers of the Michigan Academy of Science, Arts, and Letters, 9
Partisan Review, 8, 17, 34
"Part of a Novel, Part of a Poem, Part of a Play," 42
A Passage to India, 38
"The Past Is the Present," 80
Paterson, 8, 60
Pearce, Roy Harvey, 20, 161, 162
"Pedantic Literalist," 60, 61-62, 66
"People's Surroundings," 69-70
Perreault, Charles, 38, 129
Petain, Marshal, 88-89
"Peter," 27-28, 60, 64, 68
"Picking and Choosing," 25, 60, 64, 65
"Pigeons," 117
"The Plumet Basilisk," 19, 24, 50-53, 83, 94
Pocahontas, 144
"Poetry," 17, 28, 60-61, 62, 63, 64, 66, 108

Poetry, 13, 32, 36
Poetry and the Age, 77
Portsmouth, Ohio, 31
Potter, Beatrix, 151, 152
Pound, Ezra, 8, 18, 33, 35, 36, 120, 159
Pratt Institute, 15
Presbyter John, Prester John, 110-11, 114
"Pretiolae," 117
"Progress" (see "I May, I Might, I Must")
"Propriety," 115
Prose, 129-30
Prufrock and Other Observations, 35
Pulitzer Prize, 14, 38

"Queen Mab," 27
"Qui s'excuse, s'accuse," 83
"Quoting an Also Private Thought," 117

"Radical," 84
"The Rat Retired from the World," 124
Redon, Odilon, 157
"The Red Wheelbarrow," 18
"Reinforcements," 84
"Rescue with Yul Brynner," 30, 154-55
Richmond, Frederick W., 153
"Rigorists," 86, 87-88, 109, 148
Robert Frost: The Trial by Existence, 37
Rochester, University of, 14
Rodman, Selden, 108
Roethke, Theodore, 40
Romains, Jules, 34
"Rosemary," 137-38
"Roses Only," 82
Ruskin, John, 129

St. Hubert, 148-49
St. Jerome, 76, 149-50
St. Louis, 13, 31
"Saint Nicholas," 148-49, 157
Saintsbury, George, 28
St. Valentine, 149
Sandburg, Carl, 69

4 7600

811,52
121,60